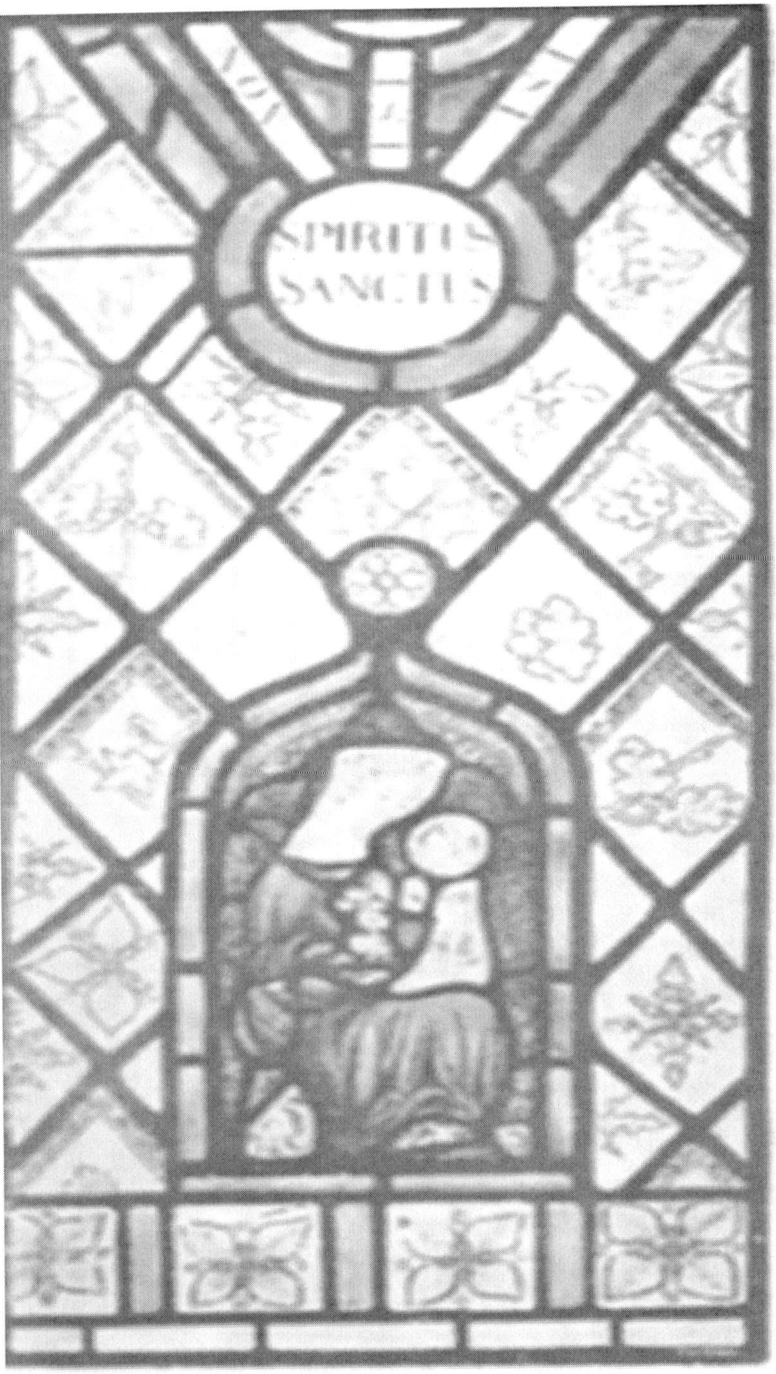
SPIRITUS
SANCTUS

ANCIENT STAINED AND PAINTED GLASS

ANCIENT STAINED AND PAINTED GLASS

KALPAZ

ISBN: 978-93-5128-713-1(HB)

First Published in 1913
Indian Reprint in 2017

Published by

Kalpaz Publications
C-30, Satyawati Nagar,
Delhi – 110052
E-mail: kalpaz@hotmail.com
Website: kalpazpublications.com
Ph.: +91-9212142040

PREFACE

THESE pages make no pretence to give an exhaustive account of their subject, but only to supply sufficient data to ground an intelligent appreciation of such remains of stained and painted glass older than 1700 as are still to be found in ancient buildings.

In the introductory chapter I have shortly described the matter with which we have to deal—in particular, its fragmentary condition and the historical causes which have produced that condition. Also, I touch upon the subject of the connection between glass-painting and the other arts ancillary to architecture with special reference to their common objects and use.

The styles, which may be taken, roughly, to synchronize with those into which English architecture from the 11th century onwards is usually divided, are then briefly described, and I have, in the concluding chapter, ventured to say a few words upon latter-day treatment of old glass, and to make some suggestions which may, I hope, be found helpful towards, not only the preservation, but also a reasonable use, of what is left.

Several of the illustrations are taken from the county of Essex, which is generally supposed to be below the average in remains of old painted glass, and I may add that it would not be difficult to illustrate all the styles in painted glass by fine specimens from Essex alone. This fact affords reasonable justification for the inference that there is, in every county in England, an open book about old painted glass which only needs a little editing—*i.e.* copying and arranging the copies in some fairly accessible place—to make it of the greatest possible value to students and craftsmen, and to the public at large.

F. S. E.

WALTHAMSTOW, ESSEX,
Christmas, 1912.

CONTENTS

LIST OF ILLUSTRATIONS

Note.—The Le Mans examples are from Hucher's Book on Le Mans Cathedral, those at Wilton, Westwell, Merton College, Kingsdown and Selling are from Winston's *Styles in Ancient Glass Painting*, the arms at Ockholt are from Lysons' *Magna Britannia—Berkshire*, and the remainder are from drawings by the writer, some of which are in the Victoria and Albert Museum, South Kensington.

Thanks are due to the Catholic Publishing Co., Ltd. and to the Editor of *The Catholic Fireside* for the loan of blocks of some of the illustrations.

CHAPTER I

INTRODUCTORY

THE initial difficulty in the way of acquiring a correct notion of the value and use of stained and painted glass is the fact that the old coloured windows—our only trustworthy guides—have come down to our time in so fragmentary a state. Take, with one or two exceptions, any old parish church in England: very seldom is all the old glass left, even in a single window. Here is a figure of a saint, there the symbol of an evangelist; in one window is a mutilated border and, in another, are a few quarries with designs of leafage, small animals or birds, or monograms.

As illustrative of this state of things with regard to parish churches, we may mention the 13th century glass in the south chancel window at Chetwode church, Bucks.; the medallion representing Henry II's penance for his part in the murder of St Thomas of Canterbury, formerly at Rollright church, Oxfordshire, and now in the Bodleian Library, Oxford; the history of St Laurence in fifty panels in the east window of Ludlow church; the *Jesse* window in the Cordwainers' chapel and the pilgrims receiving St Edward's ring from St John in the Fletchers' chapel, both in the same church, and the very fragmentary glass—a few loose pieces only—at Knowle church, Warwickshire.

The case of Knowle deserves attention, for it is an excellent illustration of the extent to which, since the 17th century, ancient glass has disappeared from our churches. When Sir William Dugdale, herald and antiquary, visited this church in 1640, he found three painted windows which had been set up by Thomas Dabridgecourt, Sir William Wigston and one Aylesbury, also, in the tracery, seven shields of arms borne by angels. By 1793 all that was left of the windows was a fragment of an inscription—these words only, "p̄ bono statu orate"—and a few fragments of saints and kneeling figures, while, of the heraldry, there remained only two shields. To-day we shall look in vain in the windows of Knowle church (which was restored in 1860) for the smallest fragment of this old glass, although it is true that a few scraps of it are kept in a box at the church.

To these we may add Shrewsbury church with its great 14th century *Jesse* window and the splendid Perpendicular church at Cirencester, where, in St John's chapel, is some 15th century glass.

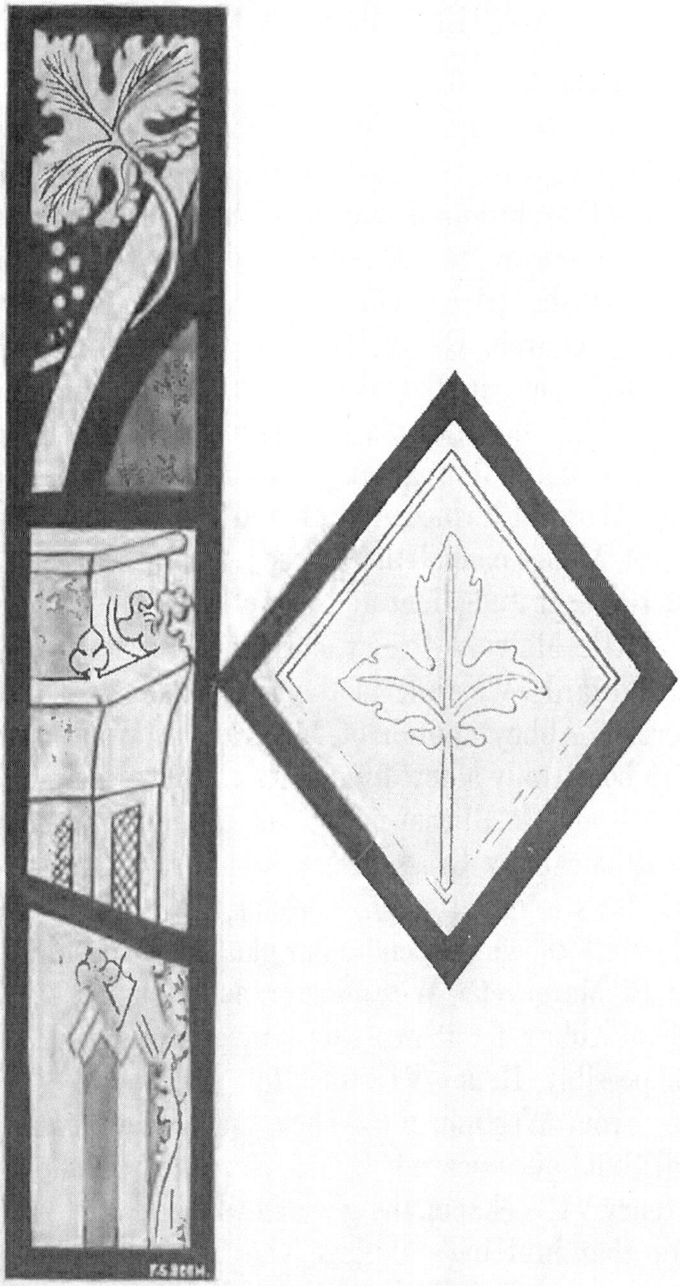

Fragment of border and quarry (Roydon)

In the remains of conventual churches we can hardly expect much old glass, for they were, for the most part, dismantled of their furniture and fittings at the Dissolution of the Religious Houses. Such of them, however, as still possess old glass tell the same tale as the parish churches. At the Benedictine Abbey church, Great Malvern, there is some 15th century glass in the aisles representing the life of Our Lord, the acts of St Wulstan of Worcester and figures of the four great Doctors of the Church and also those of Prince Arthur and Sir Reginald Bray. In St Anne's chapel there, also, we may see a picture of the Last Judgment and one of the Creation, while at Little Malvern Priory church, there is some glass of Edward IV's time in the east window. The Cistercian Abbey church of Merevale in Warwickshire can boast only a few fragments. In the magnificent nave—almost all that is left—of the mitred Abbey of Waltham Holy Cross, Essex, not a scrap of the old windows is left, though, perhaps, we ought to claim the well-known perpendicular glass in the east window at St Margaret's, Westminster, as belonging to Waltham Abbey, for it was there, by gift of Henry VIII, or possibly, Henry VII, for a few years.

From Westminster Abbey the ancient glass has all but disappeared. The clerestory windows of Henry VII's chapel, the glass in which set the pattern for that in King's College chapel, Cambridge, now contain only some fragments which were formerly in the Lady chapel; in the west windows of the aisles are other remains and, in the Jerusalem Chamber, are fragments of early 13th century glass.

At Tewkesbury a little 14th century glass is left, and, at Dunster Priory church in Somersetshire, there are, among other fragments, a pilgrim's hat with escallop-shells, and a crown, all that are left of a head of St James of Compostella and the figure of a king, which were complete in 1808. There is, also, at Dunster a quarry decorated with a pastoral staff and a scroll bearing the words, "W. Donesteere Abbas de Cliva," a reference to William Seylake, Abbot of Cleeve in 1420.

In the 18th century the glass of the great east window—a tree of Jesse—was still *in situ*, but by 1808 only a few fragments of it were left. In 1808, too, the arms of Luttrell were in a window of the north aisle of Dunster church, but they are no longer there.

In the college chapels at Oxford and at Cambridge, the loss and destruction of old glass have been, perhaps, as considerable as in the parish churches. At Oxford, the 17th century windows of University College chapel, painted by Abraham van Linge, shortly before the Civil War, have survived, and at Balliol, there are, in the side windows of the chapel, fragments of 16th century glass from the old chapel which was destroyed in 1856, while other pieces—arms of benefactors—of 14th century date, are in the windows of the lower Library. Here, in some cases, while the shields of arms have been preserved, the inscriptions under them have been destroyed, highly illustrative of the carelessness with which painted glass was formerly treated. Merton, in the side windows of its chapel, can shew the oldest glass in Oxford, that given, in 1283, by Henry de Maunsfield, who subsequently became Chancellor of the University.

In the Library of the same college is some old glass which bears testimony, in the "Agnus Dei" (the Holy Lamb), often repeated, to the former dedication to St John the Baptist.

In the chapel at Queen's College there is some early 16th century glass, which, with the exception of that in the two western windows on each side, was restored and repainted by the younger Van Linge in the 17th century and again much restored by one of the Prices in 1717. William of Wykeham's New College retains its original 14th century windows in the ante-chapel, except in the west window, where is the well-known painting of the *Nativity* by Thomas Jervais, from Sir Joshua Reynolds's cartoons.

The windows in the chapel proper at New College contain good 17th century Flemish glass, though those on the south side were largely repaired and repainted by William Price in mid-eighteenth century. Lincoln College chapel, consecrated in 1631, contains foreign glass of the 16th century, while the chapel of All Souls has much of the original 15th century glazing left, amongst which are portraits of John of Gaunt, Archbishop Chichele the Founder, and of Henry V and Henry VI.

Magdalen College, in the ante-chapel, has some 17th century glass and, at the west end, is a large window, *the Last Judgment*, of the same period, which was, to a great extent, repainted in 1794. In Trinity College chapel there is no old glass, but in the Library is a figure of St Thomas of Canterbury and other fragments.

If we add to this list the windows in the chapel at Wadham College, we shall have a fairly accurate idea of the old glass in Oxford Colleges which has survived the ill-treatment to which painted glass has been subjected from the end of the reign of Henry VIII to, almost, the present day. The Wadham chapel windows are contemporary with the foundation of the college (1613) and were all painted by the Flemish artist, Van Linge the elder.

At Cambridge, the condition of the old picture-windows is, on the whole, much the same, although there, in King's College chapel, we find an instance of the whole of the ancient glass having been preserved to the present day. In the chapel at King's the twenty-four side windows and the east window are filled with glass made and set up in the reign of Henry VIII, which is designed to shew forth pictorially the Christian scheme of religion—"the story of the old lawe and of the new lawe," as it is expressed in the contract for the making of the windows—in much the same way as the windows at Fairford church to which we shall presently come. There is, however, a variation in treatment; for, whereas, at Fairford the tale of our Lord's earthly life and of the events which led up to it are grouped together in the eastern half of the church and the history of His Church is in the western part, at King's College chapel there is no such sharp division. In other respects, however, the scheme is the same at King's as at Fairford: in particular, the east and west windows at both have similar subjects, though it should be noted that the glass in the west window at King's is not ancient, having been given in 1879 by a former Fellow of the College. In the side-chapels of King's College chapel are also, besides more 16th century glass, some figures—Apostles and Prophets, King David and Bishops—of early 15th century date brought from elsewhere; perhaps, Ramsey Abbey after its dissolution.

In the chapel (built 1632) at Peterhouse, where, it is on record, the Puritan visitors defaced six angels which they found in the windows—the east window is 17th century work, *a Crucifixion*, mainly copied from Rubens' picture of the same subject at Antwerp. At Trinity College, in one of the oriel windows of the Hall is a 15th century figure of Richard, Duke of Gloucester (afterwards Richard III) and there is much 17th century, and later, collegiate heraldry in the other windows.

If we turn to the Cathedrals—taking a few of them only—they tell, for the most part, the same story of destruction and neglect. At Canterbury, of all the painted glass with which every window was filled, we see to-day only, in the great west window, fragments from other parts of the cathedral, among them the arms of Richard II; in the end wall of the north transept pictures of Edward IV and his Queen, their daughters, the two Princes murdered in the Tower of London, and a headless figure of St Thomas which was broken by Richard Culmer—"Blue Dick," the Canterbury fanatic—in Commonwealth days. In the south transept is some glass of the Perpendicular period, and, in the north choir aisle, between the transepts, is ancient glass, probably set up shortly after 1220. This last-mentioned glass and that of about the same date, in the windows of the Trinity chapel and the Corona, which represent the miracles of St Thomas of Canterbury, are the most interesting in the cathedral. In the north-eastern transept, also, are fragments from the windows of the north choir aisle.

Of all the English cathedrals York has fared the best with regard to preservation of its old glass. Every window in the nave and aisles, except four, retains its ancient glazing. The earliest in point of date is that of the first half of the 13th century in the windows of the north clerestory. The famous "five sisters" window in the main north transept has preserved its original early English glazing. The glass in the aisle-windows ranges from early 14th century to the reign of Henry VI, and one window of the choir—the easternmost on the south side—contains 16th century glass brought from the church of St Nicholas at Rouen. The perpendicular glass of the great east window representing stories from the Old Testament and of the Last Judgment with figures of the Heavenly Hierarchy and of the Saints, is the original glazing, as is, also, that of the 14th century in the west window of the nave.

At Rochester all the ancient glass disappeared during the religious changes of the 16th century, at St Albans is a little 14th century heraldry of great interest and Chichester cannot shew even fragments of the old window-glazing. Winchester retains more, though none of the earliest period. In the west nave window is about the oldest glass in the cathedral, perhaps of the time of Bishop Edingdon (1346—1366) who built the west end. In its present state, however, this glass is very fragmentary, and is, no doubt, made up of remains of several windows. In the aisles and clerestories we find late perpendicular glass, and the glazing of the east window of the choir, except the three figures in the top tier, which are modern, may be dated about 1525. An interesting feature of this window are five shields shewing Bishop Fox's arms, impaling those of the Sees which he successively held—Exeter, Bath, Wells, Durham and Winchester—and his motto, *Est Deo gratia.* In the Lady chapel, also, are remains of old glass contemporary with their perpendicular settings.

It is commonly alleged, as the reason for the poverty of Salisbury cathedral in the matter of old glass, that the architect Wyatt, who worked his will on the old church from 1782 to 1791, broke down an enormous quantity of the ancient window-glazing and threw it by cart-loads into the city ditch. Probably he did, and it is, no doubt, also true, as is usually said, that Bishop Jewell, in Elizabethan days, removed much of the old glass. It may, nevertheless, be doubted whether these iconoclasts acted very differently from other men of their respective times, though they may have been rather more thorough in their methods than others, and, after all, there are ancient cathedrals and many other great churches with which Wyatt had nothing to do, with even slighter remains of old painted glass than Salisbury. A few scraps, however, were left, for, in 1830, the three west windows of the nave and aisles were filled with fragments of various dates from all parts of the cathedral—a proceeding almost as reprehensible as Wyatt's doings. In the great west window are some Early English medallions and fragments of a *Jesse* window of the first half of the 13th century, of a Crucifixion and some perpendicular and renaissance glass said to have been brought from Rouen. At the bottom of the three lights is a row of shields bearing the arms of England, France, Provence, the Earl of Cornwall, Clare and Bigod. In the west windows of the aisle are remains of 13th century borders and other patterns and, curiously enough, in the head of the south aisle west window, are the arms (dated 1562) of Bishop Jewell, to whom the destruction of so much of the old glass at Salisbury is attributed. In the upper lights of the east window of the south transept is some Early English glass.

At Oxford cathedral, in the Latin chapel, are three complete 14th century windows, and there is an interesting piece of work in the window at the west end of the north aisle of the nave painted by the younger Van Linge—*Jonah and his gourd.* In the south choir aisle is a reminiscence of the dissolution of the monastic houses in a 17th century window containing a portrait of Robert King, last Abbot of Osney and first Bishop of Oxford, with the Abbey in the background, while, in the east window of the south transept, is some 14th century glass, notably a panel of the murder of St Thomas of Canterbury, the saint, as is often the case, being headless.

Exeter possesses, as things go, a fair amount of old glass. In the great east window is some early 14th century glass, much of which was in the window which preceded the present one, itself as old as 1390 or thereabouts. The survivals from the older window seem to be SS. Margaret, Catherine, Mary Magdalen, Peter, Paul and Andrew; the others—SS. Sidwell, Helena, Michael, Margaret, Catherine, Edward and Edmund, and Abraham, Moses and Isaiah—being contemporary with the existing window. In the central bay of the north clerestory are four headless figures of the Early Decorated period, while in the Magdalen and Gabriel chapels is some 16th century glass. At Wells there is, probably, more old glass than in most of the English cathedrals. In the west window of the nave are figures of King Ina and Bishop Ralph of Shrewsbury of the Perpendicular period and renaissance panels representing the life of St John the Baptist, brought from Rouen and Cologne in 1670. The great east window and the two clerestory windows of the choir adjoining it are ancient (about 1340). In the east window is *A stem of Jesse* and also, in the tracery, a picture of the Last Judgment, which is continued in the tracery of the clerestory windows. In the lower lights of the easternmost window of the north clerestory are *figure and canopy* subjects, one of them St George. In St Catherine's chapel and the south choir aisle are many fragments, while the windows of the Lady chapel are filled with glass of various dates. The east window of this chapel was restored by Willement and contains two tiers of figures under canopies, in the tracery above being angels holding shields with the Instruments of the Passion. Other traceries shew an evangelist's symbol and heads of patriarchs and saints. In the Chapter House are fragments, among them the arms of England ancient (*i.e.* the lilies of France in the first and fourth quarters and the English lions in the second and third) and those of Mortimer. In the Vicars' chapel are the arms of Bishop Bubwith (1407—1424)—three chaplets of holly leaves.

These examples of the present-day condition of ancient painted glass in some old English cathedrals, churches and chapels will suffice not only to shew how comparatively little of the old glass is left in any one building, but to demonstrate the difficulty of appreciating what has been lost or destroyed.

Time was when these and similar fragments were but minute parts of an ordered arrangement for admitting light through coloured media into the building which they adorned, an arrangement which was itself a part only of a great scheme comprising the whole building and everything belonging to it, its architecture, its wall-paintings and its coloured and gilded pillars and arches, and the wood-work of roof and doors and screens. All being so richly coloured and gilt, why should the windows be excepted? They were not: the broken border seen to-day ran round the whole window, the saint's figure was part of a small picture set in the midst of a trellis of vine shoots, oak-sprigs or ivy-leaves. The evangelist's symbol, to-day probably broken, was one of four—the winged man of St Matthew, the winged lion of St Mark, the winged ox of St Luke and the eagle of St John—which filled the tracery lights where now we see the one solitary symbol. All the windows were wholly stained and painted, thus contributing to the total effect—the harmony which resulted from the unity of effort of mason, wood-carver, painter and worker in glass.

In a sense, however, this decorative or artistic effect was but an accident, though one which invariably resulted from the mediaeval craftsman's work. Primarily, the idea underlying all this unified beauty in old buildings was usefulness—the notion of means to an end. Craftsmen of the Middle Ages knew nothing of art for art's sake: their object was to produce something useful and fitting to the end in view. If their work was beautiful it was so because it answered that end and according to the degree in which it did so. Now the end to be kept in view in all work connected with a church was, to the mediaeval mind, instruction—the driving home, as it were, through the senses, of the Church's message. As paintings on walls and pillars (such as we may see to-day in many churches, notably the 13th century church of Our Lady and St Laurence at Trier and St Albans' Abbey church) shewed, to learned and unlearned alike, the story of the Church's life through the centuries, so painted windows did the same.

It follows, therefore, that any enquiry into the origin and history of stained and painted glass, if *exhaustively* carried out, must embrace very much more than that one subject. It branches out into every craft that is concerned with the history of buildings of all sorts—of cathedrals and parish and collegiate churches, of monastic houses, colleges, castles and palaces, moot-halls and manor-houses, for in all of these glass painting was used, in conjunction with the other crafts and arts, to minister to the ends for which such buildings were set up.

This notion of unity of endeavour and its results being always borne in mind, we may with advantage turn to the classical example—as it may be called—of the use to which painted windows were put in old days—the church of Fairford in Gloucestershire, where every window retains its ancient painted glass. Even at Fairford, however, we must bear in mind that owing to the destruction of much of the old internal colour—wall-paintings and such-like—we cannot correctly estimate the original colour effect of the old glass. But, although the harmony which resulted from painted wall-spaces between the coloured windows is lost, the subject scheme of the Fairford windows can still be worked out and we can see what was the teaching end for which they were adapted.

The plan of Fairford church is a nave with north and south aisles, chancel and central tower. The east end of each aisle forms a chapel, Our Lady's chapel on the north and the chapel of the Blessed Sacrament on the south. These chapels are separated from the aisles, of which they respectively form part, and from the chancel, by carved wooden screens, and the chancel-screen across the nave may be treated as connecting together the western screens of the chapels, so that the whole church may be said to be divided by screens into two parts, an eastern and a western. The significance of this arrangement in connection with the subjects depicted in the windows we shall presently see.

Since Fairford church—as we see it to-day—dates from the last decade of the 15th century, we should expect to find its windows wide and lofty, and so they are. In the north aisle there are five windows of four lights each, and in the Lady chapel are three windows, two on the north of four lights each and one in the east wall of five lights. In the chancel is a great east window of five lights divided into two tiers, and one window of three lights in the south wall, while the chapel of the Blessed Sacrament has the same window arrangement as the north aisle chapel. In the south aisle there are four windows only of the same size as those in the north aisle, an arrangement rendered necessary by the south door occupying the space which one window would have filled. Besides all these, there are eight windows of three lights each—four on either side—in the clerestory, and a large window flanked by two smaller ones in the west wall.

What are the subjects portrayed in these twenty-seven spacious wall-openings and of what practical use were they intended to be? Their main purpose was to give a pictorial representation of Christian theology. In that part of the church which is eastward of the dividing line of screens, are set forth in picture-windows the facts, as taught by the Church, on which Christianity rests, and, in the western part of the church are what may be called the inferences to be drawn from those facts, viz. the Apostles' Creed, the Church's teaching as symbolised by her ancient doctors, the Church's life as shewn forth by her saints and martyrs, and the final Judgment, the consummation of all things temporal.

It would be impossible within the limits at our disposal to attempt a detailed account of the subjects of these windows. Speaking generally, the Lady chapel and the nave window immediately outside it on the west, set forth the story of Our Lord's birth, of the events which preceded it, and of His early years, beginning with the *Temptation of Eve*, *Moses at the Burning Bush*, *Gideon and the Fleece*, and *the Queen of Sheba offering gifts to Solomon*, Old Testament types of the *Annunciation*, the *Conception of Our Lord*, *His Incarnation* and the *Adoration of the three Kings* respectively.

The last picture in the Lady chapel represents Our Lord as a child teaching the Doctors in the Temple, while the lower half of the great east window in the chancel takes up the story of the closing scenes of His earthly life—*His triumphal entry into Jerusalem*, *His Agony in the Garden*, the *judgment of Pontius Pilate*, and *Our Lord's Scourging at the Pillar*. Above these is the picture of the *Crucifixion* which occupies the full breadth of the window. In the south window of the chancel are three lights shewing *the taking down from the Cross*, *the Entombment* and *Our Lord preaching to the Spirits in Limbo*.

In the Blessed Sacrament chapel the centre light of the east window is devoted to the *Transfiguration of Our Lord* as a type of the miracle of

Transubstantiation, while the other windows shew the *Resurrection* and the principal events of Our Lord's subsequent life on earth, ending with *His Ascension into Heaven.* This long list of Christian facts, as we have called them, ends with the *Descent of the Holy Ghost upon the Apostles.*

Now for the inferences from these facts. In the first three windows of the south aisle—counting from the east—are the twelve Apostles, four in each window, and each one bearing a scroll containing a part of the Apostles' Creed. This is in accordance with ecclesiastical tradition, which teaches that, before the Apostles separated for their missionary labours, they composed this creed, each contributing a portion. St Peter, bearing a scroll with the inscription, "Credo in Deum Patrem omnipotentem, Creatorem cœli et terræ," begins the series and St Matthias ends it with the closing words of the creed "Et vitam æternam."

To balance and complement this apostolical company we find opposite to them, in the north aisle, figures of the twelve Old Testament prophets, beginning with Jeremiah, whose scroll contains the words, "Patrem invocabitis qui fecit et condidit cœlos," opposite to St Peter, and ending with Abdias (Obadiah), opposite to St Matthias, with the words "Et erit regnum Domini." So far the Creed.

There remain the westernmost windows of the

aisles. These contain, on the south, the four great Doctors of the Church—SS. Jerome, Gregory, Ambrose and Augustine of Hippo—and, on the north, opposite to them the four evangelists; thus completing what may be called the direct teaching of the Church.

Next, going aloft to the clerestory, we see results of that teaching symbolised by figures, on the south side, of saints and martyrs—Dorothy, Sebastian, Agnes, Margaret, a Bishop, perhaps St Thomas of Canterbury, an Emperor and two Kings, a Pope and two Cardinals, and, opposite to them—opposite in the moral order as well as in actual position—are twelve figures of persecutors, Annas and Caiaphas with Judas, Herod, Diocletian and others.

Last of all, we turn to the western wall of the church, where, in the centre, is a great window of seven long lights, divided, like the east window, by a transom.

In the upper part Our Lord, as final judge of all, sits enthroned, surrounded by the Heavenly Hierarchy in circles—Angels, Cherubim and Seraphim and the twelve Apostles. On the right hand of the Great Judge is a lily and, on a scroll above His shoulder, the word "Misericordia," while, on His left, is a sword, and a scroll inscribed "Justitia"—the lily of mercy and the sword of justice. Before Him kneel Our Lady and St John the Baptist as suppliants for worldlings, while the orb of the world, glowing as with fire and its buildings crumbling into ruin, is beneath His feet.

In the lower half of this window is the result of the Last Judgment, St Michael dividing the lost souls from the saved. On his right is the Paradise of the Blessed, on his left the eternal home of the condemned ones, and, around his feet, are the dead arising from their graves. On either side of this great picture is a smaller window—the northern one shewing the Judgment of Solomon, and that on the south the Judgment of David upon the Amalekite who slew Saul, both types of the final Doom between them.

The essential fact to bear in mind is that this arrangement in painted glass at Fairford is the great surviving example in the British Isles of what, in more or less varied form, we might have seen in every church, great and small, in mediaeval Europe. Small churches would compress the series, larger ones would amplify it, and its arrangement might be varied, but, certainly, in the western world, the plan was universal from the 12th century onwards. The windows of the eastern end of the church set forth the tale of the Gospel, the nave shewed the prophets and Apostles, and the west window reminded folk as they left church of the last scene of all—the Great Judgment.

The fragmentary state of old painted glass seems to be due to several causes of which fanatical violence is, probably, the least. It has long been the fashion to throw the blame very largely upon the Puritans, and, more particularly, upon Cromwell's soldiers. There is, no doubt, a measure of justice in this view, for there are instances on record of smashing of picture-windows in Commonwealth days both by fanatical civilians and by Parliamentary soldiers. Examples of the one we have in Blue Dick's rage against the painted windows at Canterbury and the fanatic Dowsing's window-smashing in the course of a journey, undertaken for the purpose, through parts of East Anglia, and of the other in the destruction of painted glass in Winchester cathedral and other great churches by the Commonwealth soldiery. But these, and similar, outbreaks were more or less isolated acts of violence and it is certain that they could not account for the disappearance of the greater part of the ancient glass throughout England. Neither is there reason to believe that Queen Elizabeth's Ordinance for the destruction of superstitious painted windows in churches was generally obeyed.

Here and there we come across instances of the intentional breaking of the old windows by church authorities—as at Long Melford, Suffolk, where the churchwardens' accounts shew a payment of 11*s.* to "Fyrmyer the Glasyer of Sudburye for defacing of the sentences and imagerie in the glasse wyndowes" —but such cases are rare.

What actually happened in Elizabeth's days was, probably, consistent with what we are told by William Harrison, himself a country clergyman, Rector of Radwinter in Essex. He was the author of *A Description of England*, prefixed to Holinshed's Chronicle, published in 1577, and he tells us, in his *Description*, that "As for churches themselves, belles and times of morning and evening praier remain as in time past, saving that all images, shrines, tabernacles, rood loftes and monuments of idolatrie are removed, taken down and defaced: Onlie the stories in glasse windowes excepted, which, for want of sufficient store of new stuffe, and by reason of extreame charge that should grow by the alteration of the same into white panes throughout the realme, are not altogether abolished in most places at once, but by little and little suffered to decaie that white glass may be set up in their roomes."

Neglect, therefore, more than violence, was the enemy of the old glass through Tudor and Stuart days, and we may safely conclude that that factor, with the restoring zeal—often ill-instructed—of the last century and a half, are together responsible for the deplorable state to-day of ancient painted glass in England.

CHAPTER II

NORMAN AND EARLY ENGLISH STYLES (1050—1272)

From the middle of the 7th century, when Benedict Biscop brought glass-workers from Gaul to glaze the windows of his stone churches at Wearmouth and Jarrow, glass, in buildings of the larger kind, was increasingly used in England in lieu of the horn laminae and oiled cloth theretofore employed to close window openings. The exact date when plain glass —itself of varied hues—began to give way to glass intentionally coloured and arranged in patterns we do not know, but, from the remains which exist in continental churches, we may infer that the glass which filled the small, round-headed windows of the churches set up in England in late Anglo-Saxon and early Norman times was coloured, and did not, materially, differ in structure and colour from that of the later Norman and Early English periods which immediately followed them.

It is likely that accidental varieties in colour, arising from the crudeness of the methods of glass manufacture, originated the idea of applying colour to glass, and it is easy to see how the idea, once formed, led to ordered arrangements of pieces of glass, diversely coloured, and how they, in time, resulted in the geometrical patterns and picture panels of the late Norman and Early English styles. It is probable, too, that the art of glass-mosaic had a part in the early development of the coloured window.

Glass wall-mosaics for interior decoration were in use in the East as early as the 6th century, and what more likely than that the glazier would think of utilising the small pieces of glass used by the mosaic worker for the purposes of his own craft? It must have been quite the obvious thing to set the pieces of glass in stucco or cement of some kind and the idea of the soft lead binding, grooved on both sides, would speedily follow. Indeed, it is said that alabaster was used in the great church of Santa Sophia, Constantinople, for glass setting.

A point to remember is that binding of some sort was a necessity for early glaziers, for glass in those days was made only in small pieces, none of them large enough to fill any but the smallest window, and we can well understand how this necessary support, as patterns became more intricate, was made to follow the outlines of the design and grew into an integral part of it. Indeed, we may say that the lead binding of a painted window, besides holding together the pieces of glass of which the window is formed, serves the same end as the black outline to figures and other objects which is an invariable feature of the miniatures and scroll-work in illuminated manuscripts of the Middle Ages.

This decorative as well as useful office of lead binding is in no style more conspicuous than in that of the earliest painted window-glass of which we have any first-hand knowledge—that of the 11th, 12th and 13th centuries. Especially is this noticeable in the geometrical and floral pattern windows of those periods.

The exactitude with which the lead binding follows the intricacies of the small patterns is largely productive of the sparkling jewel-like effect which is characteristic of early glass.

The panels, once in the Sainte Chapelle, Paris, and now in the Victoria and Albert Museum, South Kensington, shew this quality very well.

It is often said that the oldest painted windows in England are those in the Corona and Trinity chapel at Canterbury cathedral. Undoubtedly they belong to the style which we are considering and we may assume that the great lancets in which they are set, and which were finished by 1171, were originally filled with painted glass. The subject, however, of the present windows, the story of the miracles wrought by the intercession of St Thomas of Canterbury—which is shewn in a large number of medallions—

suggests a later date for them than one so near the time of his martyrdom, and we shall not be far wrong if we fix that date shortly after 1220, in which year the body of the saint was translated from the old shrine in the crypt to the new one in the Trinity chapel behind the High altar. Earlier than 1220 these windows cannot well be, for, in one of them, is a representation of the new shrine set up in that year, and it may well be that they are later in the 13th century even than 1220.

The huge "five sisters" lancets at York, too, are sometimes brought forward as rivals to the Canterbury windows in the matter of age. They, however, are made of white glass, with, comparatively, little colour in their borders, a style which came in rather later than the medallion style.

On the whole it is not easy to locate the oldest piece of painted glass in the British Isles and it is quite possible that it may be found in some of the fragmentary glass which, from time to time, has been brought from the continent—from France in particular—and leaded up in the windows of out-of-the-way rural churches. One may, indeed, though with diffidence, suggest that the four panels in the centre light of the east window at Rivenhall church, Essex, which were formerly in the apse of the church at Chénu in France, may be older than any of the original windows now existing in our churches. The

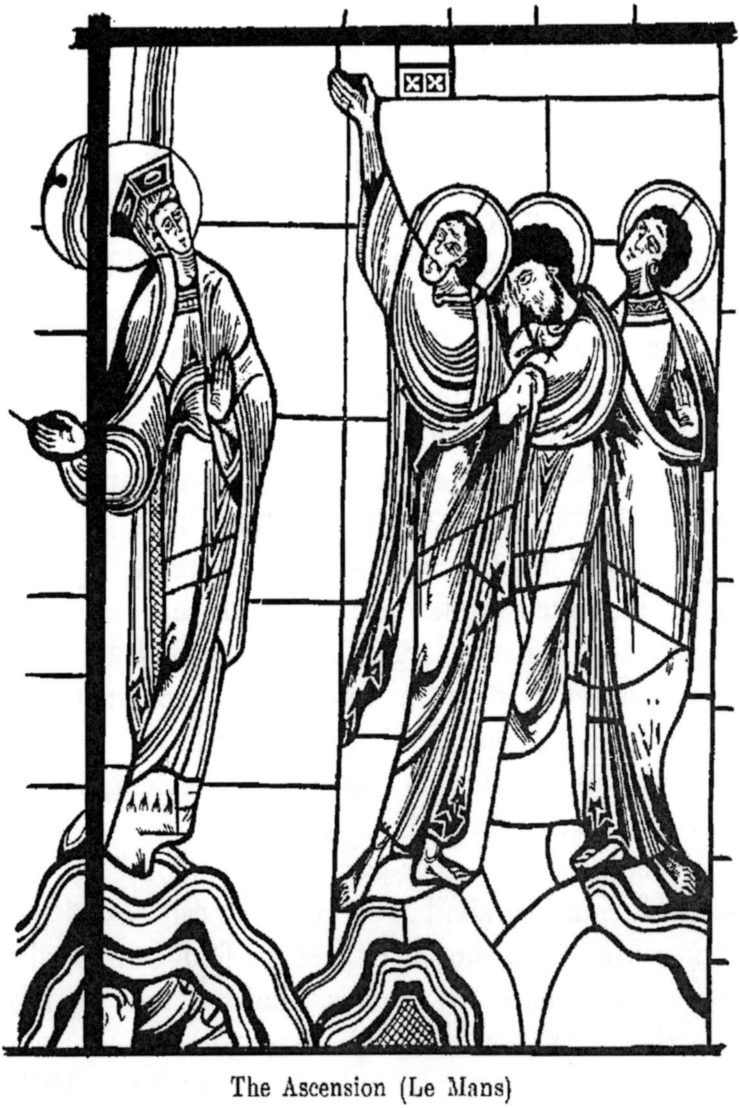

The Ascension (Le Mans)

pronounced Byzantine character of these medallions, which represent our Lord in glory, His Entombment, the Blessed Virgin Mary with Our Lord, and the Annunciation, inclines one to think that they are much earlier in date than the Canterbury windows.

However the question may stand as to our own country, it is certain that for a sight of the oldest extant painted glass we must turn to France, whence the art of glass-painting came to England. In the cathedral at Le Mans we find what we seek in one of two windows which are the sole survivors of the windows of the earlier church, which was devastated by fire in 1134 and again in 1136. This window, representing *the Ascension,* shows twelve figures, easily identified as the Apostles, looking upwards, besides the Blessed Virgin Mary—the central figure in the lower tier—who, according to the constant tradition of the Church, was present at the Ascension. The ascending figure of our Lord is absent, either because it was left to the imagination, or, as is more likely, because the upper part of the window has been lost. Judging by similar extant compositions of the 12th century, we should expect to find Our Lord's figure surrounded by angels above those of the Apostles. The date of this *Ascension* window is probably as early as the episcopate of Bishop Hoël (1081—97), who is known to have glazed the windows of Le Mans cathedral, and a great French authority,

M. Hucher, suggests the year 1090. From the facile character of the drawing, especially as evidenced by the pose of the figures, we should judge that the artist was an adept in the execution of sacred pictures according to the ancient rules of Greek Christian art. Perhaps the next painted glass in point of age may be taken to be some of that in the Abbey church of St Denis in France, the windows of which were filled with coloured glass by Abbot Suger in the middle of the 12th century.

It is necessary to bear in mind that there are two kinds of coloured windows generally recognised—pot-metal and enamel-painted. The pot-metal window is the original and the only kind usually made until the middle of the 16th century, when the use of enamel-colours for glass-painting came into fashion. Pot-metal is the name given to glass which is coloured in the course of manufacture—in the crucible or pot—and which comes to the hands of the glass-painter in the form of small sheets of coloured glass, some blue, others green and so forth. From these sheets are cut pieces of glass as required by the artist's design; say, from a sheet of ruby a piece to represent a mantle, from a sheet of blue a piece for sky, a clear white, or, in early times, a pink and sometimes brown piece for head, arms and hands.

When the design has, in this way, been made up,

the artist paints, with an opaque pigment called brown enamel, though it used to be purplish-grey and the French call it black (not to be confounded with enamel colours proper), upon the pieces of pot-metal the details of his design—the features, hair, hands, arms and feet of the figures and the folds of their garments and such-like. With the brown enamel he also puts in the shadows, using the pigment either thickly or thinly according to the density required. Thus, the only painting done by the artist is with brown enamel, the colour of the design being supplied by the pot-metal. This painting done, the pieces of glass are placed in the kiln, the heat of which makes the surface of the pot-metal to fuse just enough to cause the artist's work in brown enamel to be absorbed into and become part of, itself. When the baking is done, the pieces of pot-metal are handed over to the glazier, who binds them up, according to the artist's design, with grooved lead binding and the window is ready for fixing.

This, ignoring minor technicalities, is the story of the making of every coloured window (with a few exceptions) from the earliest times to the 16th century, and it is the way in which nearly all coloured windows have been made since the revival of the ancient method in modern times.

A word as to enamel-painting on glass for window purposes. As the pot-metal process probably grew out of wall-mosaic, so the enamel process may have developed from painting on porcelain, and it is possible that, if the use of enamel glass-colour had been known in the far-away days when the notion of coloured windows arose, the pot-metal window would never have been. This would have been a misfortune, for enamel-colours lack the brilliancy of pot-metal.

Enamel-painting is simply painting on sheets of white glass with prepared colours in the same way as one paints in oil or water-colour. Each colour—local colour, shadows and outline—is applied with the brush, a great contrast to pot-metal work, in which the local colour is supplied by the glass itself. When the picture or design is finished, the sheet is placed in the kiln and the work is completed in the same way as a pot-metal window. As enamel glass-colours were not invented till the 16th century, it is obvious that we shall not be concerned with enamel-painting until we reach that period.

It may be of interest to note that a kind of glass-painting, distinct both from pot-metal and enamel, has, from time to time, been in use, a process which has its advantage where extreme permanency is not desired. That process is painting on glass with colours ground in varnish, preferably amber varnish. This plan enables one to use every tint and every combination of tint, provided that they are transparent, for the local colours; it is applicable both to pot-metal and to sheet-glass and the troublesome and risky process of baking in the kiln is dispensed with. The effect of the baking, in the case of ordinary glass-colour, is to fix the colour to the glass, an effect which is attained, in varnish painting, by the amber medium, which, locking up, as it were, the colours in itself, adheres firmly to the glass. The writer can say from experience, that permanency, extending over many years, can be obtained by this system of varnish-painting on glass, and that the colours so treated become so well fixed and hard as to resist the action of a metal scraper. It may, therefore, be a question whether the process might not be adopted in cases where expense is a factor to be reckoned with—for varnish painting is cheaper than kiln-baked work—especially where painted windows are required for temporary churches or for domestic buildings. The process has also the sanction of antiquity, for Vasari tells us that it was used by old Flemish painters with success, and we know that the great artist *Magister Paulus*, painted some windows in this medium for the Friars Minor at Venice and that copies of them were set up at the Franciscan Friary at Treviso.

To return to the style which we have under consideration—the late Norman and Early English—all pot-metal work, of course. The earliest windows in this style are made entirely of coloured glass, for it was not until later that white glass (really greenish-blue) decorated with patterns in brown enamel came into use. These early coloured windows, which follow immediately in point of date that very old glass of which the *Ascension* at Le Mans is an example, are of four kinds:

Medallion windows,
Figures with or without canopies,
Jesse windows,
Coloured patterns.

The oldest medallion windows, those of the 12th century, ought, perhaps, to be placed in a class by themselves. They mark the transition from the Byzantine *Ascension* type to the more ornate medallion windows, such as those at Canterbury and the Sainte Chapelle, Paris. This transitional glass is very rare, and we may take, as typical of the class, a window at Le Mans cathedral which represents the story of SS. Gervasius and Protasius. In the *Ascension* type of window the divisional lines were rectangular, while in the later medallion style they were, on the whole, curvilinear. The SS. Gervasius and Protasius window shews both types. Of the centre panels some are square, others are circular, the top one is vesica-like and those at the sides are rectilinear. We also see, in the small spaces between the circular and square panels, the beginnings of those floral fillings-in which constitute so marked a characteristic of the later medallion windows. All these features are shewn in our illustration—three panels, originally in the fourth tier from the top of the window, representing the martyrdom of St Gervasius. Part of the border of the centre panel, as the illustration indicates, has been cut off in the setting, perhaps in modern times. While upon the subject of this transitional glass one is tempted to suggest that the Rivenhall panels may be of the same style.

As time went on, medallions became less square and more curved in their main lines. For as good an early example as can be found, we may turn again to Le Mans and take one of the long lancets (13th century) which set forth the life of Our Lady. Our illustration shews the top panel of this window —Our Lady crowned and enthroned in the midst of flowers and holding them in her hands, a composition which, as M. Hucher remarks, recalls that passage of the *Golden Legend*: "Nazareth means a flower; as St Bernard has said, Mary, herself a flower, wished to be born of a flower, in a flower and at the time of flowers."

Here we have square and round panels set, not one over the other, as in the 12th century, but in different lines of verticality, thus producing greater variety of outline and giving occasion for extension of

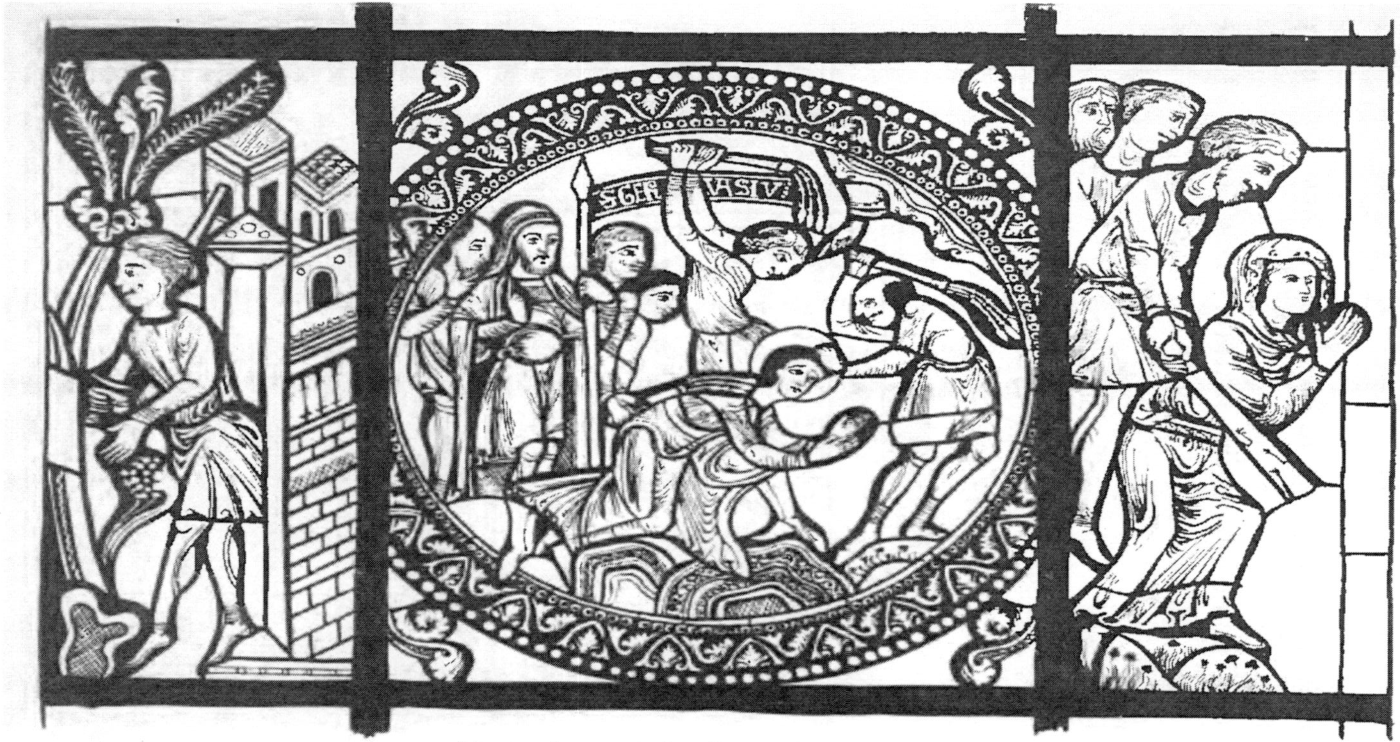

Martyrdom of St Gervasius (Le Mans)

the floral fillings-in and for the introduction of more elaboration in the backgrounds. In the base of this lancet is an interesting feature. The donors of the window, the guild of money-changers of Le Mans,

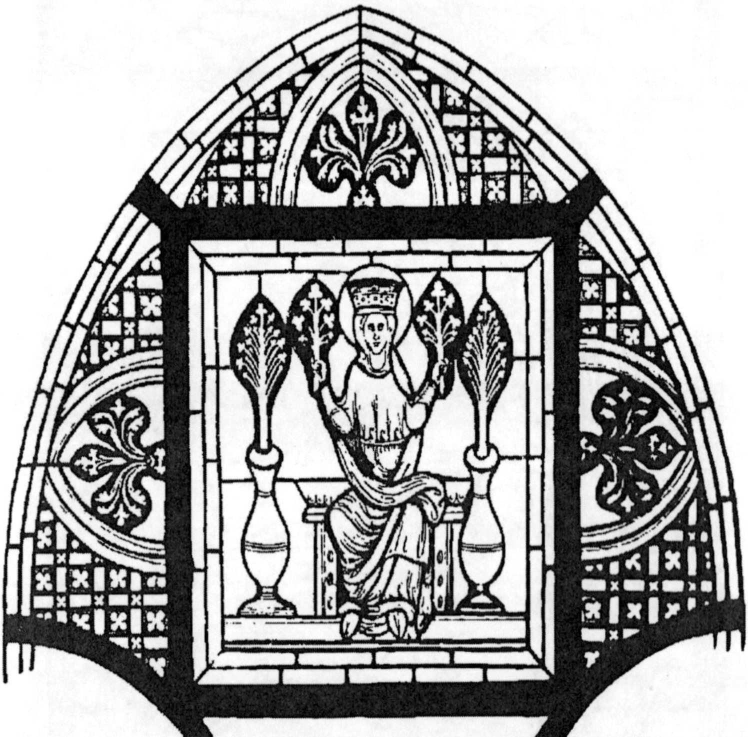

Our Lady enthroned (Le Mans)

are seen at their work. Here a money-changer is testing a coin, there one weighs money in a balance, and above these, we see others doing business with customers from whom they seem to be receiving some goblets and handing over long purses apparently full of money in return.

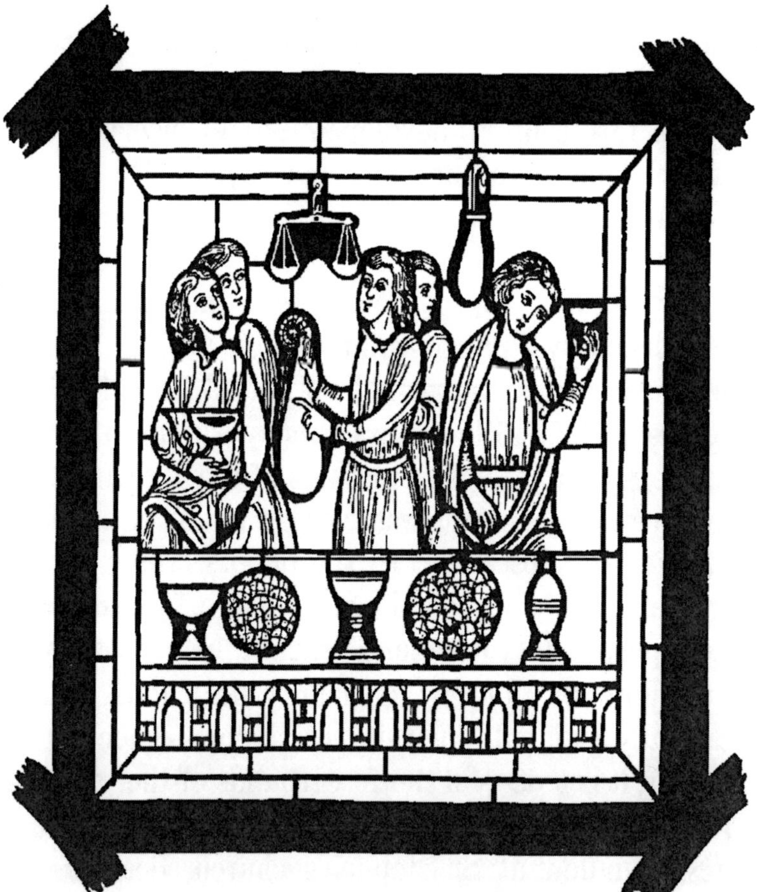

The Money-changers (Le Mans)

This is an early example of a practice, common in all periods, whereby those at whose expense a work of sacred art had been made, were commemorated in the work itself. In altar-pieces, wall-paintings and painted windows we see the same practice. Beginning, as at Le Mans and Chartres (where some thirty different guilds gave windows), with pictures of donors doing their usual work, the system had, by the 15th century, developed into an incorporation of the donor into the story portrayed. He or she would be represented in an attitude of devotion, as if actually in the presence of the holy persons shewn in the picture, and, sometimes, as in the act of being introduced by a patron-saint to their notice. Shields of donors' arms, too, would be placed beneath their figures, as in a 15th century canopy-window at St Lô. In the renaissance glass pictures of the 16th and 17th centuries this custom was carried so far as to make the picture subservient to the donors, whose figures are painted disproportionately large. Interesting examples of this decadent practice may be seen at the church of Montfort L'Amaury near Paris, where carefully painted portraits of donors—kneeling in prayer, it is true—fill the foregrounds of the pictures. Perhaps an extreme instance is the 16th century *Jesse* window at St Stephen's church, Beauvais, in which portraits of reigning kings are introduced as blossoms on the genealogical tree. Onwards from the early part of the 16th century inscriptions, with or without coats of arms, were often substituted for the figures of donors. This practice is illustrated by the little panels from Baden now in the south window of the chancel at Lambourne, Essex and by the four fragmentary windows, survivors of many, one of which bears the words, "Thys wendow made be the good man Thomas Francys 1526"—at South Mymms, Middlesex. As the object of all these forms of commemoration of donors was to remind posterity to offer prayers for their souls, none of them occur in England from the days of Philip and Mary to the revival of Catholicism in the 19th century.

The 13th century medallions became gradually more and more complex in design, the square panels disappearing and the circular ones becoming quatre-foiled, while background patterns became yet more elaborate. Another example from Le Mans—the adoration of the three kings—shews this very well. At Tours cathedral, also, are very similar designs made up of vertical rows of quatre-foils in the centre with side-rows of semi-circles. In all these later medallion windows should be noted the closeness of the lead binding and consequent smallness of the pieces of glass which, together, help to produce the jewel-like effect to which we have before referred. Also, it should be remembered that, in this style the panels are set in iron bars, indicated in the illustrations by thick black lines.

The St Thomas windows at Canterbury may be taken as typical of the fully developed medallion style, and they afford the best, and very available examples in England for study of 13th century glass of this character. Their panels are of all possible shapes and their fillings-in and borders are very elaborate. They and the glass from the Sainte Chapelle in the Victoria and Albert Museum will amply satisfy a desire for first-hand knowledge of late medallion windows.

Speaking generally, the use of coloured, to the exclusion of white, glass is characteristic of the early medallion style. Necessary contrasts were obtained by using light colours on dark, as *e.g.* light-coloured figures on a dark background or *vice versâ*, and when, as in the case of the Canterbury windows, white or very light glass is extensively used, it is a sign of late work.

It is obvious that 13th century medallion windows would have a tendency to exclude light. Little or no white glass and much lead binding would, together, ensure this. While the dim light thus caused is agreeable enough at the floor-level of a great church, we need, as a corrective, brighter light from above.

Therefore it was that the clerestory windows in the 13th century were usually, but not always—as witness the clerestory medallion windows in the choir at Tours cathedral—glazed in a totally different style from the main windows. The idea being to admit light, single figures of great size—often under low canopies—the make of which would allow of the use of large

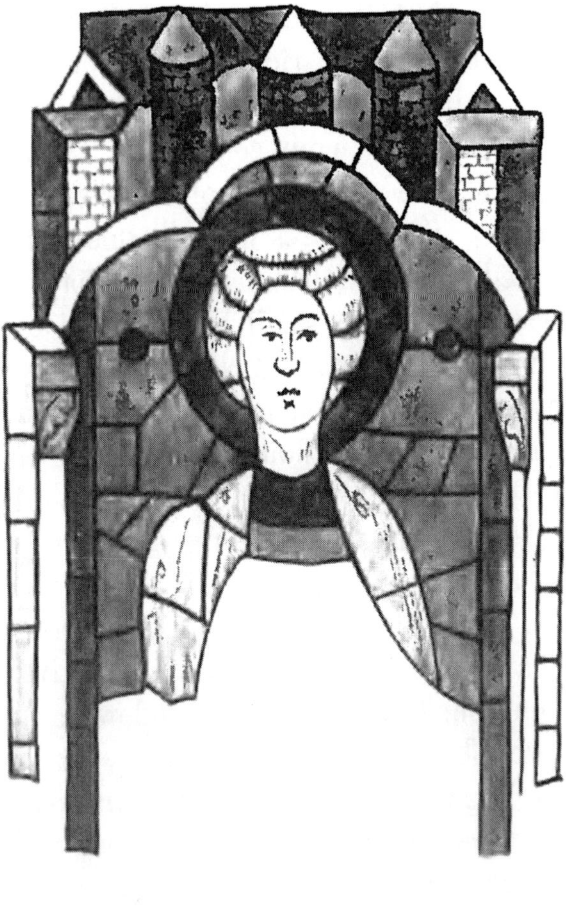

Fragment of figure and canopy. Wilton. (13th century)

pieces of glass, were inserted in the clerestory; in

each window, as a rule, one figure, but sometimes two, one above the other. At Canterbury, in the clerestory of the Trinity chapel, were such figures as these representing the Old Testament ancestors of Our Lord; but they are gone. Similar figures, however, noticeable for richness of colour in their dress and in backgrounds and borders, may be seen in the clerestories of many continental churches; in particular, at the cathedrals of Chartres, Rheims, and Bourges. Such figures were, in this style, sometimes placed elsewhere than in the clerestory. Several of them, each under a small low-crowned canopy—both figure and canopy being richly coloured—would, one above the other, fill a tall lancet. To this class also belong figures without canopies on white or coloured grounds, of which the gigantic St Christopher (30 ft. high) at Strasburg cathedral may be taken as an example.

While in France the medallion type continued in use long after the single large lancet had given place to the mullioned and traceried window—as witness the Sainte Chapelle in Paris, built by St Louis in 1248—in England it was given up when mullioned windows were introduced. Then came the white windows, so-called, though they were not without colour here and there, especially in the borders. The finest specimen in England is the *Five sisters* window at York cathedral, five great lancets, with clustered mullions between them, occupying the whole width of the end wall of the north transept. At Salisbury cathedral are five, unhappily, mutilated, windows of the same class, though earlier in date than the *Five sisters*, as is partly evidenced by the greater quantity of colour in the borders.

At Westwell church, in Kent, is an interesting example of a small white window, made up of quarries (panes) decorated in brown enamel set in a white and coloured border. Bits of colour, too, are scattered about the quarries. Sometimes such coloured pieces are developed into panels containing pictures or shields of arms, as in the east window of Chetwode church, Bucks. In connection with these white windows we may notice, in late specimens, the beginning of a practice, which became common in the Decorated period, of placing a row of figures under low canopies (like the Wilton example) horizontally across the lower half of a window.

Thirteenth century *Jesse* windows might, perhaps, be classed as medallions, for they are designed upon similar principles. In both kinds we have small pictures or single figures in panels the subjects of which have relation one to another. In the case of the *Jesse*, however, the panels are visibly connected by branches of a tree, the stock of which springs from the side of a recumbent human figure in the base of the design. A *Jesse* window then, is

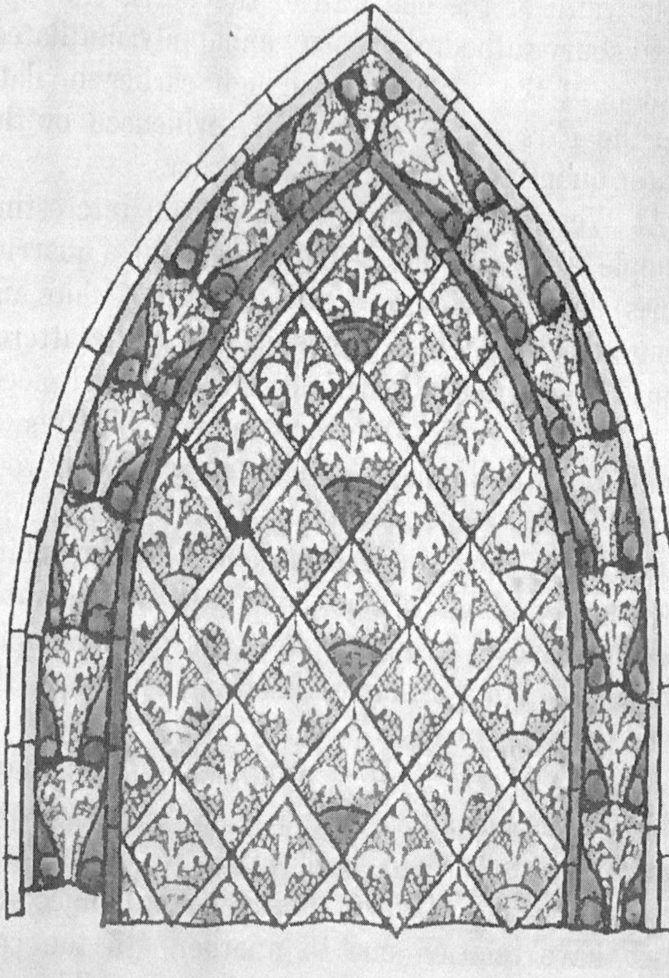

White window (Westwell)

simply a genealogical tree, in the form in which family pedigrees have been drawn from very early times, shewing the earthly descent of Our Lord, as set forth in St Matthew's Gospel, from Jesse, the father of King David, through the Patriarchs and the Kings of Judah. The number of such ancestors varies with the size of the window and the period; in the early *Jesse* at Chartres cathedral there are four only, all kings, while, in later examples, there are as many as fifty. In 13th century *Jesses* the figures are seated, holding the branches of the tree with both hands, while, in the latest examples (16th century), they are, usually, half-length figures issuing from flowers. Most of the continental cathedrals, notably Chartres and Beauvais, can shew 13th century *Jesse* windows or fragments of them, and in England, besides remains of *Jesses* of the same period at Canterbury, York, and elsewhere, there are many panels, more than is generally supposed, which have once been parts of such windows, scattered up and down the country in out-of-the-way churches. An example is the central of the three lancets already referred to at Westwell church, Kent, which contains fragments of panels shewing pictures in the life of Our Lord, a distinct variety of the *Jesse* window, and it may, perhaps, be the case that the Rivenhall panels belonged to the same type. *Jesses* are usually, or have originally been, in eastern chancel windows or in north or south walls of transepts, and very often, as at Westwell, in a central lancet flanked by *white* windows.

As to the coloured-pattern windows, such as we see at St Denis, they are rare, and, as is the case with the mixed white and colour pattern, which grew out of them, there are no known examples in England. The predominant colours in the Early English period were red and blue, the red or ruby very streaky and the blue sapphire-like in colour, either very deep or very light. The yellow was cold and greenish in tone, very unlike the bright hue of the yellow stain introduced in the 14th century. For flesh tints pink, or even brown, glass was used. The glass itself was thick, and, also, uneven, a circumstance to which it owed some, at least, of its sparkle.

The 11th, 12th and 13th century figures, like all well-designed figures intended to be viewed from a much lower level than their own, were disproportionately tall, and, of some of them, those of the later period, may be characterised as stiff in drawing; nothing can be better than the easy pose and swing of the earlier ones: as witness the figures in the *Ascension* at Le Mans.

One feature of the glass of this period should be noted: the floral ornaments are purely classical in design. This fact, illustrating, as it does, the great doctrine of evolution as applied to the arts, shews that the early glass-painters had received the artistic traditions of ancient Rome and Greece and proves that glass-painting, in those early days when first we hear of it, was no parvenu, but had legitimately developed along the same lines as the other decorative crafts from the works of the great artists of antiquity. We shall see better the significance of this matter of orderly development when we come to the 16th century.

CHAPTER III

THE DECORATED STYLE (1272—1377)

THE story of painted glass, in so far as it has developed along legitimate lines, has been a continuous one. There is no moment at which we can say that one style has ended and another has begun: change is gradual, the leading features of the one style fading imperceptibly into those of its successor. This is in the nature of things: the lives and daily work of those craftsmen who have lived in the last days of a style survive the date at which it is commonly said to end. They go on using glass of much the same texture and tone, their colours and methods of work change little, but all the time the tendency is towards variation, mainly in details. In this slow fashion the Early English style melted into the Decorated, till, at last, we get the late 14th century window with its masses of white and yellow glass contrasting with great splashes of colour—figures, shields or picture panels—scattered about its surface.

Although we could easily assign any such window to its proper style, and, with equal certainty, tell the approximate date of a 13th century medallion window, we should find the task of tracing the steps which led from the earlier to the later window a long and intricate one. The laws which govern the evolution of the works of man, like those which deal with natural phenomena, are, for the most part, slow and gradual in operation: the cataclysmic has little share in progress.

The earliest of the many influences which brought about the change of style from Early English to Decorated work seems to have been a tendency to naturalism in the drawing of flowers and leaves. At first sight, there is but little difference between the border of the white window at Westwell and that at Roydon shewn in our first chapter. A second glance, however, shews that the coloured ornaments (features of both designs) vary considerably in treatment. The Westwell design is stiff and conventional while the other, especially the stalk, is natural.

So gradual indeed was the change, that it was not until the first decade of the 14th century was nearing its end that any readily noticeable difference in style was apparent. About that time two causes—one the result of orderly development and the other of an accidental discovery—combined to produce distinct variation from the Early English type. First, the naturalistic school developed rapidly: exact copies of foliage—oak, ivy, vine, maple—took the place of the conventional leaves, modelled on classical examples, of the Early English period. Nor did naturalism stop here, for the leaves were made to spring from tendrils and branches issuing from a central stock. The fruits, too, were shewn—acorns, ivy-berries or grapes. Foliage such as this was made to run over the white glass the leads of which were arranged in geometrical form—reminiscent of the Early English period. To complete the naturalistic idea, bands of double lines—sometimes patterned and coloured yellow—followed the course of the leads, so that the branches of the tree or vine seemed to run in and out of a trellis, a circumstance which has given name to such windows—trellis windows. Very complete examples are in the side windows at Merton College chapel, Oxford. We may here notice the unfortunate treatment which many trellis windows—notably at Exeter cathedral—have received from would-be restorers. Either from ignorance of the original character of trellis windows or from disinclination to the trouble necessary to restore them properly, when broken or fragmentary, their irregular-shaped quarries have been cut up into pieces, all of one shape and size, and leaded up so as to form a window of lozenge-shaped quarries. Sometimes, indeed, they have been mixed up with quarries originally lozenge shaped, decorated with conventional designs, of a later date. Of this sort of muddle our frontispiece affords a specimen.

Though slow and orderly change is the ordinary law of development for the arts, it happens at times, though comparatively rarely, that rapid change in style or workmanship is brought about by an unexpected event. Such an event was the discovery, in the early years of the 14th century, of the fact that chloride of silver will impart to white glass, when heated in the kiln, a brilliant yellow stain, varying in tone, according to treatment, from bright lemon to deep orange. The value of this discovery can best be gauged by taking one's stand before a large 14th or 15th century window and trying to understand how it would look if all the yellow were banished from the canopies, floral ornaments, pedestals, monograms, shields and so forth which form the background to its main features. At once

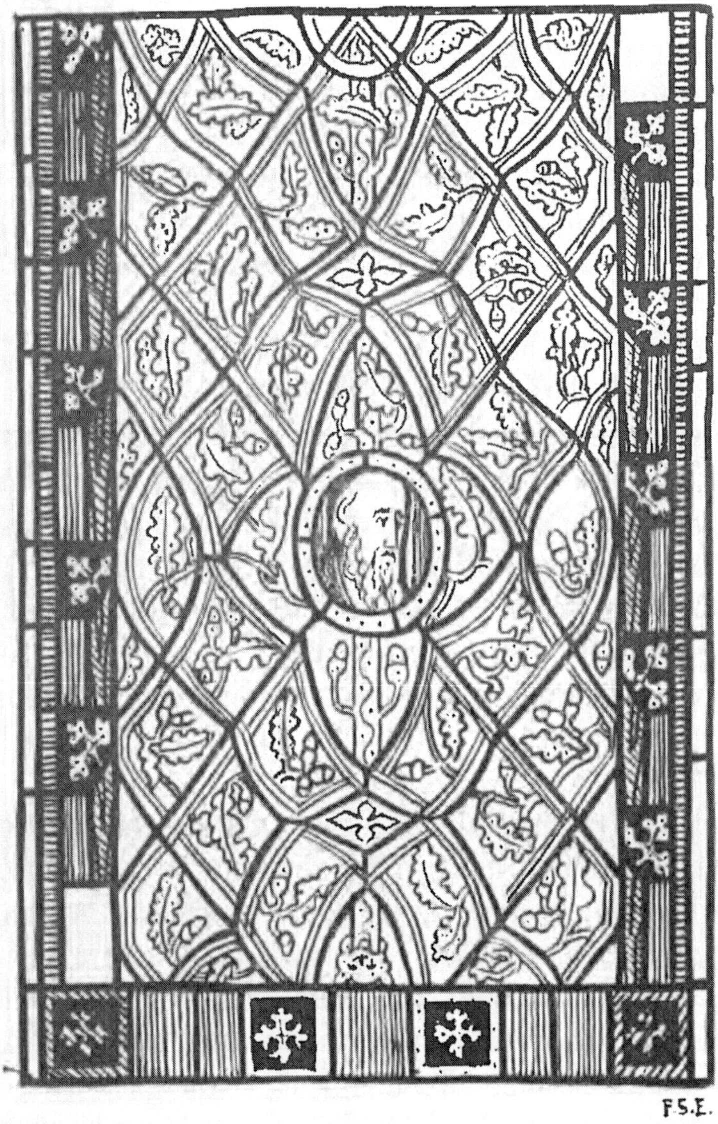

Trellis Window (Merton College, Oxford)

we see that the result would be hardness and coldness, and we come to understand that it was the discovery of the yellow stain—whereby an artist was enabled to impart warmth to his outline designs on white glass—which made these great windows, mainly composed of white glass, so pleasant to the eye. For, although yellow glass coloured in the crucible—pot-metal—was in everyday use centuries before the yellow stain was discovered, it could only be used—like all pot-metal glass—by cutting from the sheet pieces of the size required and fixing them with lead binding into their places in the design. Try to appreciate the loss of light and increase of the appearance of weight which would result from the substitution of pot-metal yellow, with its leaden binding, for every bit of yellow stain on white glass in such a window as we have supposed. The result would, probably, be an approximation to an Early English mosaic-window.

The yellow stain came just at the right time, for architects were making the divisions between lancet windows ever narrower, thus, in effect, throwing several windows into one, and, as a natural consequence, creating a demand for a lighter and brighter style of coloured glass than had hitherto been the fashion. To this demand the glass-painter responded with his white backgrounds made up of quarries decorated with delicately painted designs in brown enamel, heightened with yellow stain, which, while they admitted a sufficiency of light, at the same time mellowed it and served also to throw into relief the masses of colour in which the stories that the windows told were enshrined.

These stories were, as a rule, strictly in accordance with the scheme to which we referred in the first chapter, and with the position in the church of the windows in which they were placed. In the early years of the style they would be in panels set in a background of white glass heightened with yellow, while single figure subjects—such as Apostles, Prophets and Saints—would be under canopies, mostly white and yellow, though often partly coloured. The figures themselves would form distinct masses of bright colour, and when, as was usually the case, they stood side by side—one in each light—they formed a belt of colour right across the main lights of the window. Hence, such windows as these are called *belt windows.* Often, as in the aisle windows at York, we find, in this style, two belts of figures under canopies with small coloured panels, in the centres of the white glass intervals, containing either shields of arms or small ornamental designs. In the case of one belt only the coloured panels are seldom found and the whole background is white and yellow. Another kind of arrangement common all through the Decorated period, was that of small figures under canopies, one above another, the white and yellow of the canopies making a set-off to the bright colour of the figures.

In small windows, such as north and south chancel-lights, we find the whole space taken up by a single figure under a canopy, with small pictures, often of the donors of the windows, beneath the base upon which the figure stands. Sometimes, the base was a grassy mound picked out with flowers, as in the St Edward at Stapleford Abbots, or, more usually, a black and white chequered pavement, but there were no pedestals until quite the end of the style, when it was passing into the Perpendicular period.

An important factor in the formation of the Decorated style was the extent to which, by the beginning of the 14th century, the use of tracery in the upper parts of windows had developed. All through the style the space occupied by tracery, in the case of large windows, continued to increase, so that we often find nearly one-half of a late Decorated window taken up by tracery. The task of the glass-painter was to fill tracery lights in a way that would harmonise with the glass of the main lights. This he did by making his tracery-glass white and yellow when the lower lights were either wholly of that kind or when there was but one belt of bright colour across them. When, however, there were two colour belts the tracery lights also were coloured, thus

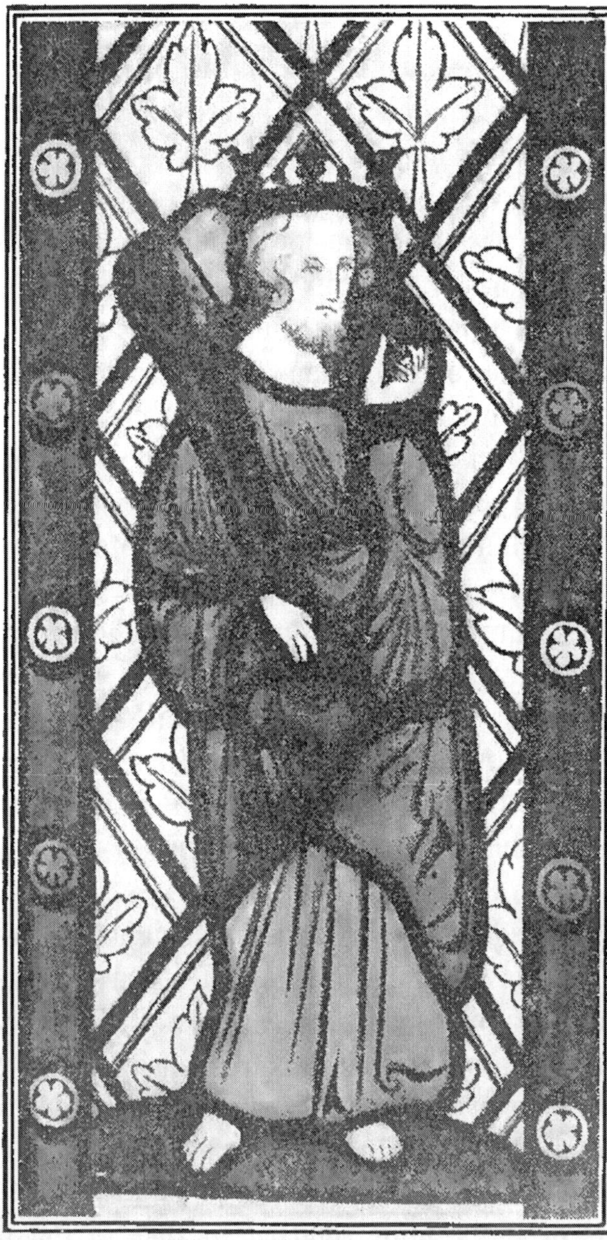

St Edward, K. and C. (Stapleford Abbots).

preserving a balance between the upper and lower parts of the window. An interesting point to be noted in this connection is that we, sometimes, find Early English glass in the tracery over glass of the Decorated period in the lower lights. In such cases the stonework of the window is Early English, and, the original glass of the same period in the lower lights having been broken, or, for some reason removed, Decorated glass has been inserted in its place. This kind of thing happened at all transitional periods. A curious example is the east-window at Sheering church near Harlow where the very elaborate late Decorated tracery (about 1370) is filled with contemporary glass representing the coronation in heaven of the Blessed Virgin Mary, while, in the lower lights, we find glass of quite recent date. Another instance is the five-light perpendicular east-window at Dyserth church, Flintshire, in which the tracery is filled with mid-15th century glass, while in the main lights is a 16th century *Jesse-tree.*

The gradual elaboration and heightening of the upper parts of all architectural features—window-traceries, canopies and tabernacle-work in general—in the Decorated period, is responsible, too, for a similar change in the canopies over figures in painted windows. The tendency (often, in this style, carried to great excess) is always towards disproportionate height of the canopy relative to that of the figure beneath it. Another feature of the canopy-window, which becomes noticeable as the Decorated style advances, is the practice of making the lower of two belts of figures and canopies subordinate to the upper one, so that, while the lower canopies are fairly low, the upper ones range aloft into a central tower and spire, with which side-pinnacles, springing from the pillars of the canopy, are connected by flying buttresses. Both spires and pinnacles are usually on a coloured ground. While, in early Decorated work the crockets and finials of the pinnacles and spires are stiff and formal in design, they develop later into graceful leaf-like forms. This was in sympathy with contemporary architecture and is another proof of the close connection which subsisted, during the Gothic period, between architecture and its ancillary crafts.

Figure and canopy-windows (a term usually confined to windows with high lower lights containing figures under very lofty canopies) were, speaking generally, although there was no positive rule, placed at the ends of buildings and high up, while the side windows were filled with white and yellow pattern glass, either alone or with belts of canopies or panels. Similarly, great variety of practice exists—no doubt expense was an important factor—with regard to the relative amount and distribution through the building of white and yellow pattern and coloured glass. In some cases, especially in small rural churches, all the windows, except, perhaps, the east-window, would be filled with white and yellow glass alone. An interesting example is Bradwell, near Witham, where much fragmentary original glass remains *in situ*. Another instance is the east window of the north aisle at Hornchurch in Essex, where the monotony of the white pattern quarries is broken by a picture of the Crucifixion in the middle one of the three main lights and by a shield of arms, surrounded by a narrow circular border, with ruby fillings-in between the shield and the border, in each of the side-lights. An opportunity for colour is found, also, in the border running round the three lights, which consists of yellow lions' faces on a white pattern ground alternating with pieces of plain blue glass. In the tracery, which is wholly white and yellow, is a picture of St Edward, King and Confessor, who belongs, in a special sense, from his connection with Havering-atte-Bower, to Hornchurch and its neighbourhood. The arms in the shields are those of Deincourt and the window, no doubt, commemorates the foundation of a chantry by a member of that family at Hornchurch. We may safely assume that the chantry altar stood beneath the window and that the east end of the aisle was partitioned off by screens to form a chantry chapel, a very common custom, and, in most cases, a reasonable one, for such an arrangement usually means that the founder of the chantry has built, or rebuilt, the aisle at his own expense.

A kind of treatment, which may, perhaps, be called *the triptych*, appears later in the Decorated period in England, although it is found much earlier on the continent. The principal subject, under a great canopy, occupies the three centre lights and smaller pictures, under canopies, are in the side-lights. The pinnacles of the canopies are on coloured grounds and, above them, is a white and yellow background reaching up to the tracery, the glass in which is coloured.

Jesse windows—which may be said to be the earliest form of design extending over the whole window—in this style have their main lights bordered and, running over the white and yellow patterns with which they are filled, and often extending to the tracery, is the vine, from which, at intervals, spring branches arranged to frame the oval panels in which are the figures of the genealogical chart.

Decorated *wheel windows*—a type which developed from the earlier *Rose* windows, from which also it seems likely that the idea of elaborate tracery in the heads of lancets arose—usually contain one or more pictures or shields of arms in their centre or eye, while the radiating lights, or spokes of the wheel, contain patterns on coloured grounds with or without borders. The east-window at Merton College, Oxford, is of this sort, the *eye* being filled with heraldry and ornamental patterns on a coloured ground.

As time went on and the methods used in glass manufacture slowly improved, the texture and character of the glass changed. It became thinner and its surface more regular, a change which was not wholly advantageous, for it is certain that much of the brilliance of very old glass is due to the varied angles, caused by unevenness of surface, at which light is transmitted through it. To improvements in manufacture also were, probably, due the gradual reduction in thickness of the coat of colour on ruby glass. Unlike other glass colours, ruby has always been applied as a surface colour, flashed on—as the phrase goes—to the glass, and the thickness of the coat of colour is found, by comparison of ruby glass of different periods, to vary as much as $\frac{1}{8}$ of an inch in the Early English period as against $\frac{1}{32}$ of an inch in the 16th century. The streakiness, too, a marked feature of very early ruby glass, tends to disappear during the Decorated period and other colours tend to vary. In particular, although there is a great deal of very dark-blue Decorated glass—dark, that is, on close inspection, though brilliant enough when viewed from a distance and in a mass—a very beautiful light-blue, light-violet, cobalt, one might approximately call it, came into use in this period.

A good example of this light-blue is the border round the little picture of Our Lady and the Divine Child in our frontispiece and of a dark-blue, of Decorated style, in the diapered backgrounds to some of the figures in the Sheering tracery.

Pot-metal yellow gets deeper in tone, passing, sometimes, through orange to a green-brown yellow —not always quite pleasant to the eye when seen in a lump, as witness the fragmentary canopies at North Weald church.

Another change of this sort to note in the Decorated period is the tendency of white glass towards a slight green tone, the result, to some extent, of its being thinner. White glass, too, definitely took the place of the pink, sometimes brown, of the Early English style for flesh tints. Its coldness was relieved by applying yellow stain for the hair and beards of figures, and when white was used for draperies, the surface was varied and warmed by yellow edgings, ornamental bands or floral ornaments, as in the mitre and chasuble of the little figure of St Edmund of Canterbury at Abbess Roding.

The white quarries in which the coloured figures and panels were set, call for a word. These were either all of one uniform lozenge shape and size or of such varied shapes and sizes as the geometrical patterns into which they were formed determined.

Of the geometrical type with their running trellis patterns we have already spoken. As to the lozenge quarries, the designs on them, outlined with brown enamel, and, after 1410 or thereabouts, usually heightened with yellow stain, varied extensively. Sometimes they were floral designs, like the maple-leaf at Roydon, or birds, as the bird playing on bells in Upper Hardres church, Kent, or family badges, monograms of benefactors and such-like. Some, too, had bands on the upper sides, either plain or patterned and with or without yellow stain. Early in the style we find quarry designs set off by cross-hatching on the ground behind them as in the Early English period (see the Westwell window), but this plan was gradually replaced by the use of the yellow stain for shading and obtaining contrasts.

Diapering of this period invites notice. A diaper is a flat pattern on a white or coloured ground, and diapering was used extensively in all the decorative arts and crafts during the Middle Ages. As limited to painted glass—pot-metal work—the diaper always consists of brown enamel applied to the glass in one of two ways. The earlier plan, which prevailed until late in the Decorated period, was to cover the glass with a fairly thick layer of brown enamel, and then, with a stick, knife or other convenient instrument, remove so much of the enamel as was necessary to form the pattern. In this way ornamental borders to garments were picked out, and background patterns, like that immediately behind the figures in the

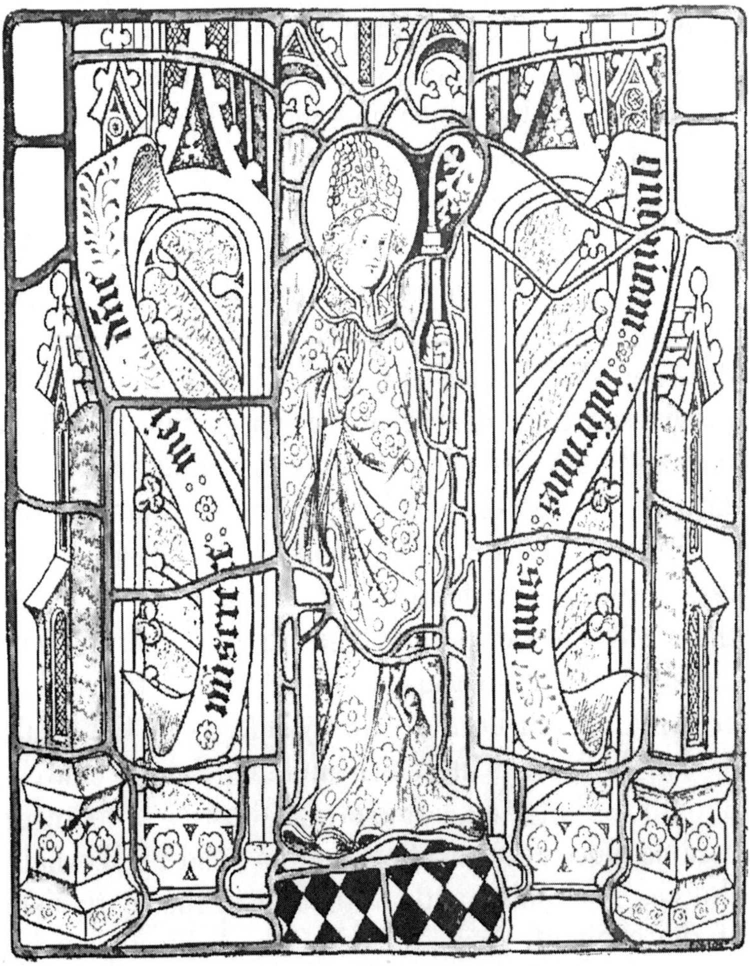

St Edmund, Bp and C. (Abbess Roding)

frontispiece, were formed. The other, and later, method, which has, since its introduction, been used side by side with the earlier one, as convenience might dictate, is simply to paint with a brush, in the ordinary way, the diaper pattern in outline. It is obvious that either plan has advantage over the other for certain kinds of work, and it is sometimes hard to tell by which method a diaper has been applied. Particularly is this so in the case of large leaf patterns, such as those on the ruby and blue grounds behind the figures at Sheering.

A typical feature of the Decorated style is the pose of the figures: they are simple and severe in drawing, the outlines becoming thinner as the style progresses, their draperies are loose, wide and flowing, and they are, usually, in constrained positions, seeming to rest on one leg. A good example is the St Edward at Stapleford Abbots. In early Decorated work facial features are treated much as in the Early English period: the iris of the eye is not distinguished from the pupil and the mouth consists of three curved dashes side by side, as in the heads of Our Lady at Kingsdown and All Saints' church, Stamford. Later on, however, the drawing of features became more natural: first, as in a head at Worfield church, Shropshire, and in another in the south aisle of the choir at York cathedral (both illustrated by Winston), the lips were drawn in outline, and, subsequently, we find both lips and the iris indicated, a development very well shewn in the tracery figures at Sheering. No very great change from the preceding style in the painting of hair is noticeable,

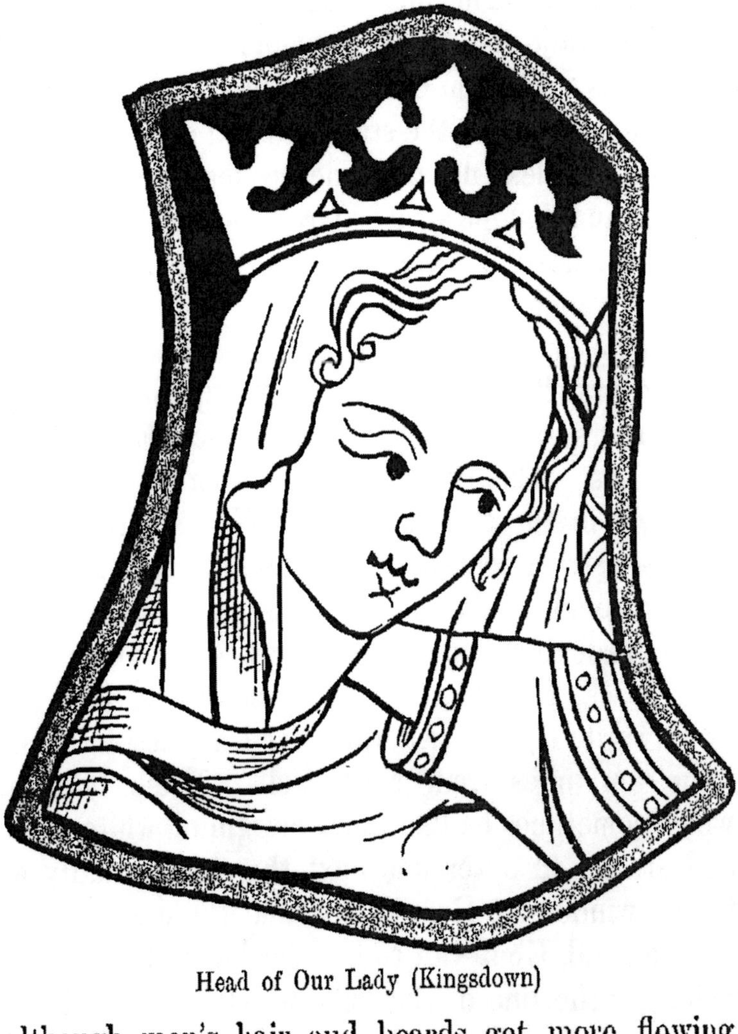

Head of Our Lady (Kingsdown)

although men's hair and beards get more flowing as the style advances, while women's hair remains long and smooth and that of angels is usually drawn in thick, crisp curls. Decorated borders must not be forgotten. The most common type is a yellow running stalk and leaf on a coloured ground: sometimes—as at Merton College, where the stalk is green on a ruby ground—the stalk and leaf are of different colours. A less usual border is made up of small figures and canopies, one above another, such as we see in the nave of York cathedral. Variety is sometimes given to the running floral border by little grotesque creatures climbing up the stalk or sitting on the branches. Heraldry often supplied material for borders—small shields of arms, merchants' marks or badges. The fragments of border in the west, formerly in the east, window at Netteswell church, Essex—ostrich feathers, alternately blue and ruby, stuck through scrolls—are remains of a heraldic border which probably had some reference to Thomas of Woodstock, Earl of Gloucester and Essex, fifth son of Edward III, who generally lived at Pleshy Castle, some ten miles from Netteswell. These borders, which sometimes had an inner margin of white glass, and always an outer one next the stone, usually, as in the window at Hornchurch, and the west window at Snodland, Kent, ran round the head of the light, following the line of the foils, which often enclosed a rose, marguerite or other small flower. If there were a border along the bottom of the window—

and often there was not, for the space would be taken up by the base of a figure-stand or by a lettered scroll—it would be of a different pattern, usually large squares containing conventional floral ornaments stained yellow on a white ground alternating with oblong pieces of coloured glass. The Merton College window and the frontispiece illustrate this practice.

The 14th and 15th centuries saw the heyday of heraldry: it was then very real, both as science and art, and, as a result of such reality, heraldic representations had then a simplicity and dignity which those of subsequent centuries lacked. In the 14th century we see no crests, elaborate mantlings or grotesquely shaped shields, only shields of the heater type, upon which were painted, in plain, bold style, a single coat of arms, a husband's arms impaling those of his wife, or at most, and very rarely, two or three quarterings. The two shields in the Hornchurch window are good types, though these are painted only in brown enamel and yellow, the shield at Westonbirt church, Gloucestershire, is another, and yet others are the four shields in a window of the north aisle of the nave at St Albans Abbey, containing the arms of Edward III, Edward the Black Prince, Lionel, Duke of Clarence, and John of Gaunt; in North Ockendon church the arms of England (ancient), Warrenne, Pointz and Beauchamp, and at

Arkesden church Fitzalan quartering Warrenne for Thomas Fitzalan or Arundel, successively Bishop of Ely, Archbishop of York, and, in 1396, Archbishop of Canterbury.

As guides to the subjects represented, figures often bore scrolls inscribed with names—*Scs̄: Petrus, Scs̄ Eduardus, M(ary) Cleophe* and so forth—and, sometimes, the names would be written round the outer edge of a saint's nimbus or, oftener, on a broad scroll beneath his feet. At times too, such scrolls would be drawn across the sides of canopies and would bear verses from the Psalter, as in the picture of St Edmund at Abbess Roding. Inscriptions up to about 1340 were in Lombardic characters, a variation of Roman letters, but, after that time, they are usually in Gothic or black letter, although Lombardic letters continued in use for a long time. Owing to the fact that Roman letters, in the long run, again came into use in Europe and so continued to the present day, it has come about that most people find it easier to read a pre-fourteenth century inscription than one of the two following centuries.

The simplest and earliest form of decoration in tracery lights was the small coloured circlet enclosing an ornament—such as a rose—painted in outline with brown enamel on white glass. This style, in its richest and most elaborate form, is found in the large foiled circles of early Decorated tracery. In such an example the centre of the light is filled with a shield of arms or a complicated floral design in colour, which touches the cusps, while within the foils are scroll-like leaves in outline, heightened with yellow on white glass. A very beautiful example of such a circular ornament is the design in the west window at Netteswell, which was, no doubt, taken from a tracery-light. The centre is light olive, delicately diapered and the narrow outer border is probably meant to be ruby, but each of its four parts are of different tints of bluish and reddish purple, an interesting result, it may be surmised, of defective firing of the glass. Nevertheless the effect is very good. As Decorated tracery progressed, its openings got higher and gave opportunity for figure-subjects which were, usually, white and yellow on coloured grounds and sometimes under canopies. The Sheering window may again be referred to for an unspoilt example of a piece of such figure-tracery and as shewing, too, the most usual kind of border for tracery-lights—the beaded type with an outer margin of white glass.

The bonnet-like crown of the Early English period grew, in the Decorated style, into the familiar circlet with floral decorations, such as that on the head of Our Lady at Kingsdown, and this, as the style advanced, passed into the more elaborate types seen on the heads of the two central throned figures at

Sheering. Similarly, the low-triangular episcopal mitre, like those worn by St Birinus and his consecrator Pope St Honorius in the Early English glass at Dorchester church, Oxfordshire, became, in *later* Decorated work, the higher and rounder shape worn by St Edmund at Abbess Roding.

CHAPTER IV

THE PERPENDICULAR STYLE (1377—1547)

COLOURED glass of the Perpendicular period, like the stone-work in which it was set, grew, by a perfectly natural process, from the style which preceded it. As Decorated tracery, having attained, in its flowing lines, such flexibility of appearance as to border on weakness, called for a corrective—found in the gradual verticalising of its principal lines—so painted glass of the same period passed through a similar phase. The flowing vine and ivy tendrils, and the natural leaves and berries of the Decorated period, which harmonised so well with their contemporary architecture, would have struck a discordant note if set in the midst of the severe lines of Perpendicular tracery. So we find that, as the 14th century passed into the 15th, the regular and hard lines of lozenge-shaped quarries took the place of the flowing geometrical patterns of the trellis windows, and the natural leaves of ash, maple, ivy and so forth, made way for conventional floral ornaments. This, be it noted, was quite legitimate development—a merely corrective process called for by a tendency to excess of flexibility—and, in no sense, a going-back upon, or departure from, the essential principles of Gothic art.

This strengthening tendency in design was accompanied by a gradual change in colour and technique: tints became softer and less intense, and facial outlines and features were drawn with finer lines and greater finish. The practice, begun, as we have seen, in the Decorated period, of indicating the iris of the eye as distinct from the pupil and of modelling both lips by fine wavy lines, became the rule. Great attention, too, was paid to shading of the face, which was done by extremely fine hair-like lines of a wavy character, much like the shading used for indicating mountains and water in a steel-engraved map.

The reduction in tone of coloured Perpendicular glass was not wholly, nor perhaps so much due to actual lightening of colour in the process of manufacture, as to greater breadth of treatment and an increase in the proportion of white glass.

Speaking generally, coloured glass was used in larger pieces than in the preceding styles, a fact which, even alone, would effect an apparent reduction in intensity of colour. Added to this, there was

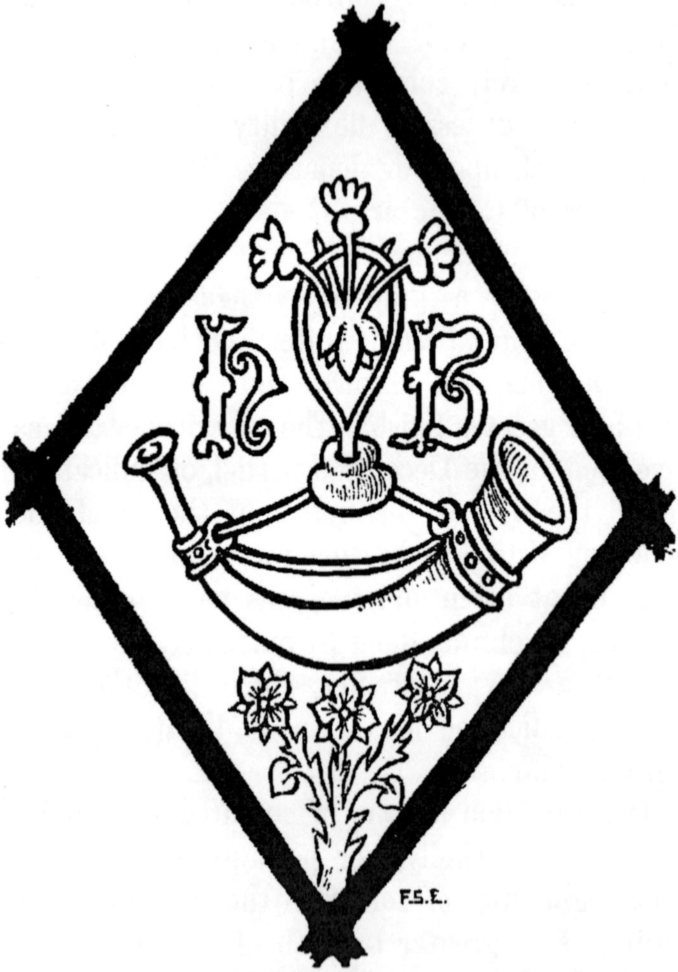

Perpendicular Quarry

a decided and progressive increase in the use of yellow stain in the white glass: we no longer find, as we did in the Decorated period, pot-metal colours used in the canopies, except for the little windows in

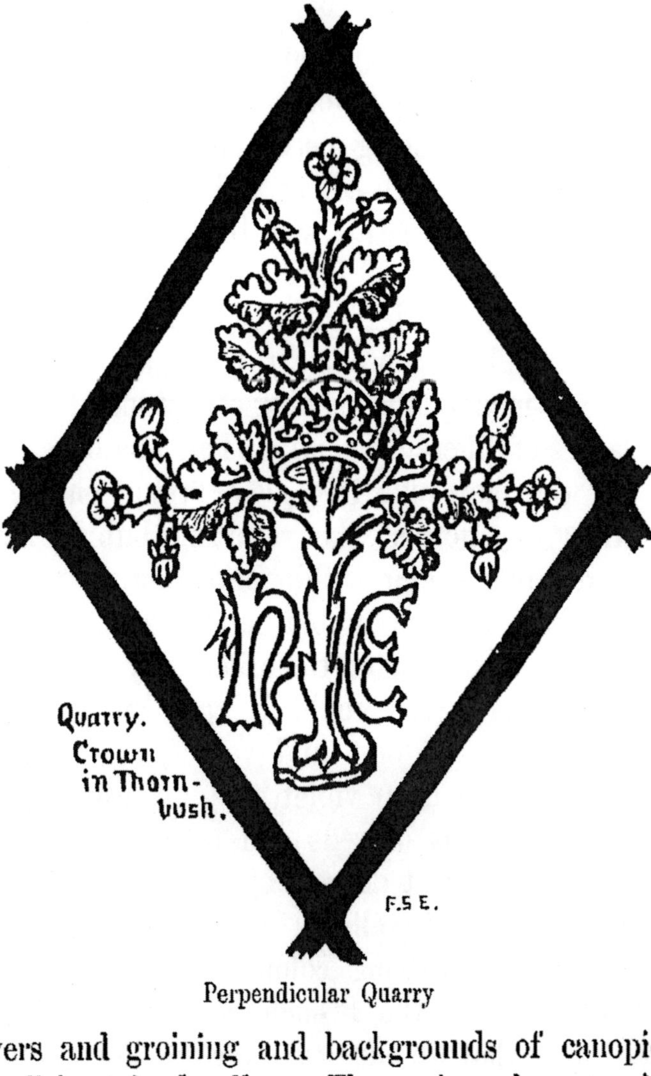

Perpendicular Quarry

towers and groining and backgrounds of canopies, but all is stained yellow. The rectangular quarries, too, in which the coloured pictures—figures and canopies or panels—are set, have more yellow than before; they are often edged with yellow and the little designs painted on them—flowers, birds, monograms, badges or what not—are sometimes entirely stained, instead of being merely shaded, with yellow.

In connection with colour, it is to be noted that the Perpendicular period saw the full development of a practice which had been introduced early in the 14th century (though, for a long time, little used), whereby the glass-painter's list of colours was greatly increased—namely, the making of pot-metal glass in two layers of different colours. This was effected by dipping the blow-pipe into glass, first of one colour and then of another, the resulting bubble being, of course, one colour within and another without. When opened out the bubble became a double sheet of one colour imposed on the other. By this process many tints of green could be got by combining different shades of blue and yellow, a long range of purples, from deep violet to pink, would result from combinations of reds and blues of varied intensity, and different degrees of orange could be got by coating red with yellow. The glass produced by this plan of increasing colour-range in pot-metal work is called by the French *verre doublé*, and it is to France that we must turn for the best examples of it. The central east windows at the church of

Eymoutiers, near Limoges, which contain many-hued canopy lights of late 15th century work, are instances in point, and the fine and elaborate canopy-window, the gift of Jacques Cœur, Treasurer of France in the days of Charles VII, at Bourges cathedral is another. As might be expected, glass-painters were not always content with two layers in *verre doublé*, and, in their eagerness for new tints, they would fuse together into one sheet five or six layers of different colours. It seems possible that this practice may have contributed towards the development of the idea of painting in enamel colours, which became a recognised system in the 16th century.

Another feature, the beginnings of which are to be found in the Decorated period, developed rapidly in the early years of the 15th century—the practice of stipple shading. Such shading—in drapery and so forth—as had been employed in the earlier styles had been either smear shading, that is a wash varying in depth with the degree of opacity required, of brown enamel, or cross-hatching with the same pigment. The difference between the new plan, the stipple and the old one, the smear, was in the method of application. Instead of a broad wash applied with the side of the brush, the painter put in his shadows by continuous dabs with the point of the tool, so that, really, they were made up of minute dots running one into the other. Obviously very much finer and wider gradations of tone could be produced by the stipple than by the smear, and we can quite understand how the increased use of stipple shading, combined with greater variation in outline, had much to do with the higher finish and air of refinement characteristic of Perpendicular work. Thus, while Perpendicular glass lost in intensity of colour it gained in culture.

At the same time the tendency to warmth of tone produced by finer shadow gradation and the consequent increase of verisimilitude of subject, were not without a bad effect, in the long run, upon the art of the glass-painter. They led, at last, to forgetfulness of essential limits and of the proper use of painted windows and to attempts, which led to the temporary ruin of the art, to paint pictures on glass in the same way as one paints pictures on canvas or paper, thus changing the very nature of a painted window by making it a mere screen upon which to show pictures instead of a coloured and decorated medium for the admission of light.

The *figure and canopy* subject, common in the Decorated period, may be called the typical style of Perpendicular times. The constructional features of the canopies are in accord with contemporary architecture: the flat-fronted Decorated canopy makes way for the Perpendicular one with projecting front; and, while the canopies of this style are of the same general character as those of the Decorated period, they are more varied in form and never run to the high pointed spire characteristic of the Decorated type. A noticeable point with regard to Perpendicular canopies is that, when there is one figure only in a main light, the whole space, except that covered by the figure, is taken up by the canopy, the pillars supporting it and the pedestal upon which the figure stands. A good idea of this sort of arrangement may be got from a study of two of the main lights of an aisle window at Fairford. This window contains figures of the four great Doctors of the Church, SS. Jerome, Gregory the Great, Ambrose and Augustine of Hippo, the two selected for study being SS. Ambrose and Augustine. The whole surface of each light is white glass heightened with yellow stain, except the groining of one of the canopies and the curtains behind the figures, all of which are red, and the copes (blue) and the tunicles (green) of the figures. The canopies, it will be noticed, which reach to the top of the lights and have pendants, differ in detail: that over St Ambrose is three-sided and more elaborate than St Augustine's, which is two-sided and broader in treatment of detail than its fellow. The figures, like all those in the aisle windows at Fairford, stand on pedestals, three-sided, decorated with foliage work about the stems and bearing, round the base, the name of the saint represented. In the tracery lights are figures of St Apollonia, St James and an angel.

Sometimes Perpendicular canopy subjects have small figures of donors kneeling in prayer round the base of the pedestal. A fine example of this is to be seen at St Lô, Normandy, in a lofty Early French lancet window of four lights which was evidently reglazed in the 15th century. The canopies, white and yellow upon coloured grounds, reach to the tops of the lights and are unusually lofty for Perpendicular work, a circumstance due to the early character of the stonework. The two centre figures only are upon pedestals, the others standing on pavement in the Decorated style, but they are all alike in that the pictures below the figures rest upon moulded bases. Under the first figure is a picture of Our Lady seated with the Divine Child on her lap, and the others have figures of donors kneeling upon tesselated pavements which form the upper parts of the moulded bases. Upon the fronts of these bases are shields of arms, heater-shape, and three other shields, supported by angels—the centre one, bearing the arms of France (modern, *i.e.* three lilies only on a blue field) —in the spandrels between the heads of the lights.

In windows divided by transoms each tier of lights is treated separately; each light has its own figure and canopy on its pedestal or pavement over a picture panel or shield of arms, as the case may be. Often, however, each main light of a window—sometimes very lofty—has a series of figures and canopies one above the other. Such windows are arranged upon the same general plan as the Decorated *belt* windows, but the canopies are loftier and the figures stand on pedestals, which grow, as it were, out of the canopy-tops.

In the Sainte Chapelle at Riom, in Auvergne, are seven fine four-light windows which illustrate this type. In one pair of lights we see the Apostles, with scrolls bearing sentences from the Creed (as at Fairford), standing on pedestals in front of curtains hanging in loops. In the canopy-tops are small niches, containing figures, probably of donors, which run upwards into another tier of pedestals, figures and canopies, and so on to the tops of the lights. Below the Apostles are canopies over figures of saints on pedestals, each of whom is presenting a kneeling figure—a donor, no doubt—to Our Lord, who is seated on His mother's knee under the first of the row of canopies. In this style, which is less common in the later years of the Perpendicular period than in its beginning, we sometimes find coloured picture-panels without canopies or pedestals, divided horizontally by panelled tabernacle work.

In all these—figures and canopies and panelled arrangements—the tracery lights shew either small figures of saints, sometimes under canopies like many of those in the Fairford windows, or symbols of the Evangelists as at Netteswell, or shields of donors' arms or those of the emperor, a king, or other eminent person of the day. A favourite tracery filling was an angel, perhaps playing on a musical instrument, or in an attitude of adoration, or maybe supporting a shield of arms.

On the continent, especially in Germany, Switzerland and Northern Italy, round quarries, set close together in rows, are, at this period, often found in lieu of rectangular quarries, as backgrounds for figures, and canopies and panels. The round quarries are, at first, about four inches in diameter with the bull's eye very well defined and with narrow rims. Afterwards they got larger, ultimately as wide as six inches, and the bull's eye became hardly noticeable.

The earlier type made a simple and effective window, especially, as was usually the case, when the surface was broken by little stars in circles made by inserting coloured glass in some of the interstices between the quarries. Round glass windows were bordered, the early ones with coloured designs and the later mostly with white and yellow only. Excellent examples of round glass are to be seen in the church of St Mary of the Capitol, Cologne, where there are several three-lighted windows with coloured subjects set in round quarries.

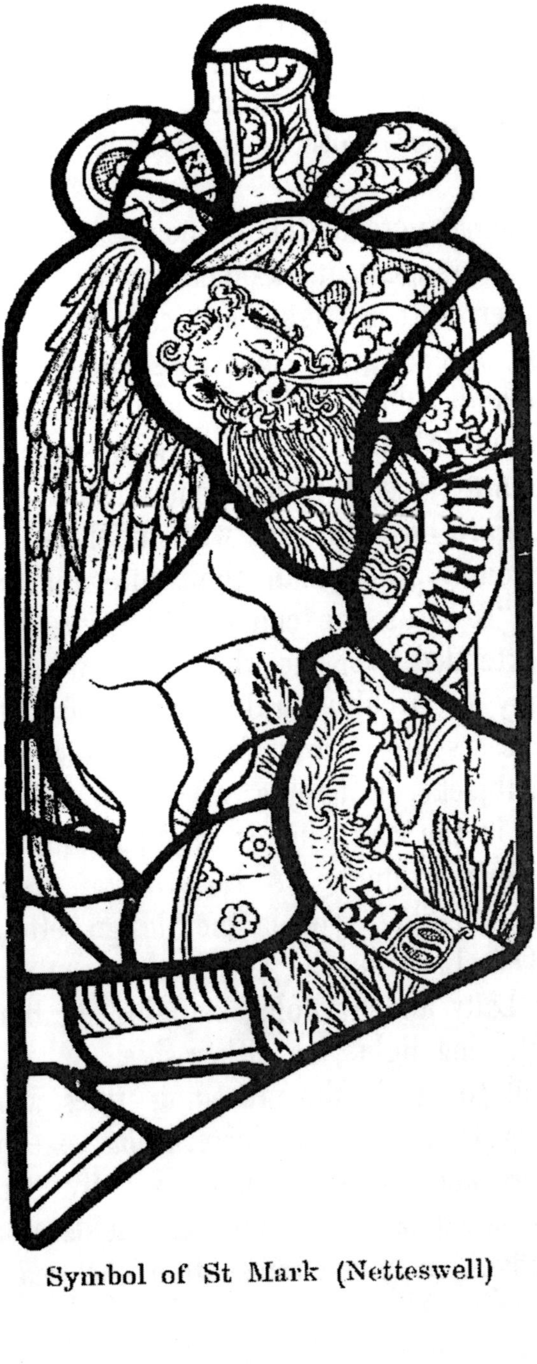

Symbol of St Mark (Netteswell)

6—2

In some, the coloured subject is in the centre light only, while in others it extends to the side lights.

A principal note of the Perpendicular period is variety in arrangement. Sometimes a centre light has a larger picture—figure and canopy or panel—than the other lights, sometimes such a central subject stands alone in the midst of a window otherwise made up entirely of white and yellow glass, or, as at West Wickham church, Kent, we see a single figure on a bracket without either canopy or background other than the white and yellow quarries. Towards the end of the style, a single subject, extended over the whole window and without canopy or architectural work, is often found. In other cases, the lower lights comprise several distinct subjects or figures, all under one large canopy, as in the east window of Winchester cathedral—an early example. A variation of the single figure on a bracket type is the design, often met with, of Our Lord on the Cross in a centre light with Our Lady and St John, standing on brackets in the adjoining lights, on either side.

We find, too, as in the preceding styles, windows wholly of white and yellow pattern glass except for the borders and variously—more usually, perhaps, circular—shaped panels containing shields of arms, crests, badges, or monograms often enclosed by a wreath, all of which are coloured. A fine, bold example of such a design, a crest within a wreath, is to be seen in the staircase-window at No. 3 Crosby Square, Bishopsgate, an old house now, and for many years past divided into offices, but formerly residential. The crest is a hawk jessed and belled painted in brown and yellow on white glass, within a green and ruby foliaged wreath.

A peculiarity of the later Perpendicular *wheel-windows* is the concentration of the coloured glass in circular bands towards the outer edge of the window and in the eye, leaving a broad circle of white glass between the two masses of colour.

The *Jesse* design of the earlier part of the Perpendicular period (of which the east windows at Gloucester cathedral and Winchester College chapel are good examples) differs little from the Decorated type. The figures, sometimes standing and at others seated, usually bear their symbols and have their names on scrolls. The vine runs over the whole window and its leaves are white and yellow, though warmth is given, in some instances, by colouring the ovals and in others by making the ground of the lights red and blue alternately. In the later examples the vine is more branched and has more leaves, the ground is usually coloured and the figures either stand on the branches or issue, as demi-figures, from large blossoms. The colouring of the leaves, too, is more varied, being often in pot-metal colour. Sometimes the vine is spread only over the two or three centre lights leaving the side-lights for other subjects.

An almost perfect "Jesse," which is dated MCCCCCXXXIII, is in the chancel window at Llanrhaiadr, Denbighshire. This window has features both of the earlier and later types. The figures in the centre light are full-length and standing, while those in the side-lights are all demi-figures issuing from blossoms. On the whole, however, the work points to a late date in the Perpendicular period, and there seems little reason for the suggestion, which has been made, that the date on the glass is incorrect. It is true that the costumes of the figures are earlier than the days of Henry VIII, but this may well be accounted for upon the supposition that, either the painter copied from earlier sources or worked in the style in which he was brought up. Changes in style are slow, and when we remember the predominantly Gothic character of the Fairford glass and that (though in a less degree) in King's College chapel, Cambridge—the one executed only about thirty years earlier than the date given for the Llanrhaiadr window and the other almost contemporary with it—we need not reject 1533 as the date for this *Jesse* on the ground of a difference between the costume of the figures in the glass and that of folk of Tudor times. A curious circumstance, which may have a bearing upon the question as to the true date of this glass, is that the original inscription upon the scroll over the head of King David—"Orate pro bono statu Roberti Jonnes, clerici qui hoc lumen vitrari fecit"—which, upon close inspection, can be made out, has been altered to "Misericordias Domini in æternum cantabo. R. J." The explanation, probably, is that the same Robert Jones—perhaps he was the parson of Llanrhaiadr—who set up the window in 1533 and who caused the erased inscription to be written, in after years, most likely in the days of Edward VI, out of deference to the then prevailing notions, had the inscription altered to the form in which it is to-day and added thereto his initials—"R. J." Such alteration of inscriptions on sepulchral monuments, brasses especially, was not at all uncommon in the troublous days of Edward VI, although it is believed that this Llanrhaiadr example is a unique instance of erasure of an inscription on glass and the writing of another in its place. When it was desired to change an inscription on glass, the piece of glass itself would, as a rule, be taken out of its setting and another piece inserted.

We have referred to the practice of placing figures of donors in painted windows. The origin of this custom seems to have been two-fold, first to indicate the personal devotion of the giver of the window, and secondly by calling him to the recollection of others, to claim a place in their prayers, for his good estate, if alive, and for his soul's weal were he dead. The same idea, no doubt, prompted the painting of coat-armour in church windows, for we find, in early window heraldry, that the arms depicted were always those of benefactors to the church or of very high folk—the king or a great local lord—whose arms, being well-known, might serve to indicate a date. As the 15th century went on, the tendency was to increase the size and importance of the figures of donors. This we may see by comparing the little donors in the base of a Decorated window with, say, the large and very beautiful figures in the early 15th century Rose-window in the north transept of Le Mans cathedral. There are seven principal figures of donors at Le Mans, all of persons contemporary with the building of the north transept and most of them known to have contributed largely to its cost. They represent Louis II of Anjou, King of Sicily and Count of Maine, who died in 1417, his wife Yolande of Aragon, his mother Mary of Brittany, and his son Louis III of Anjou, or, possibly, his second son, "the good king René"; Louis, the Bastard of Maine; Peter of Savoisy, Bishop of Le Mans (1385—1398); and Cardinal Filastre, Cathedral Dean of Rheims

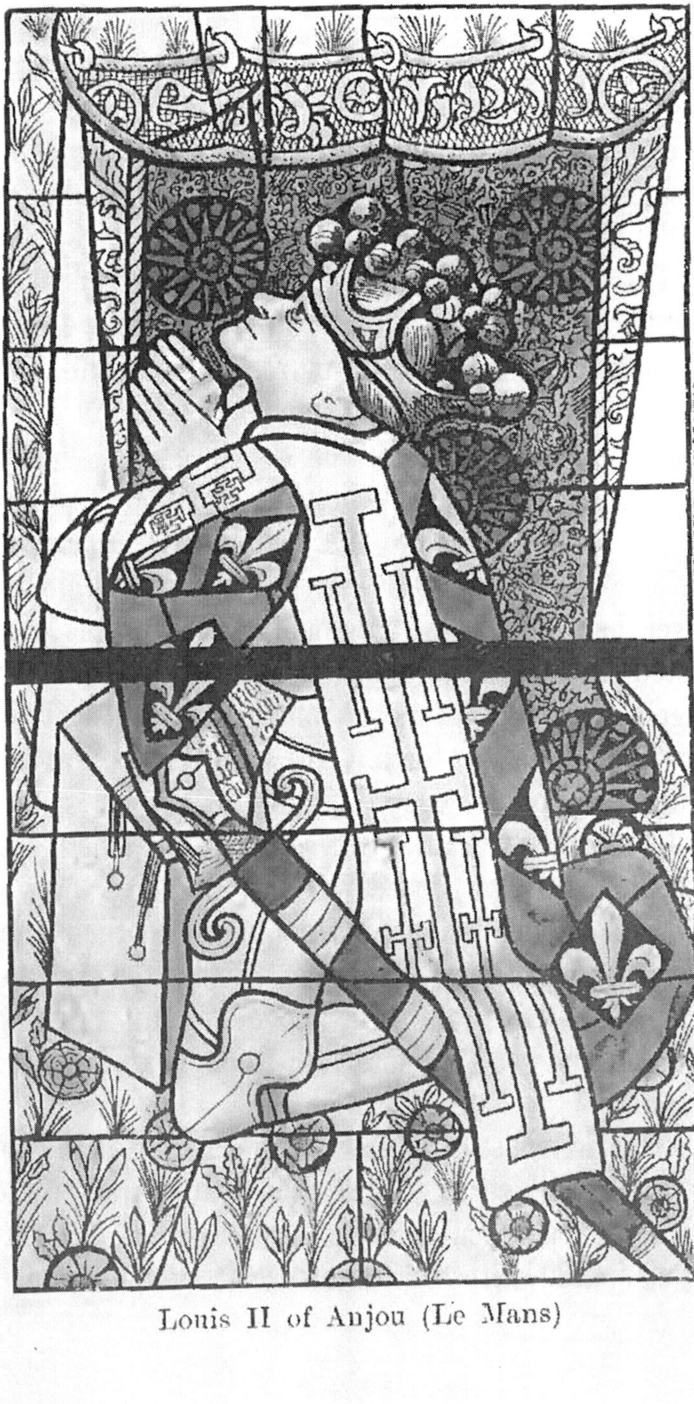

Louis II of Anjou (Le Mans)

(1411—1428), a great lover of art and letters and a generous contributor to the cathedral of Le Mans. Besides these are figures of unknown canons, donors, no doubt.

This window at Le Mans, the stonework of which is a fine specimen of Flamboyant architecture, is in two main divisions—a great rose above and long lancets below, the two connected by elaborate flame-like tracery. In the eye of the rose are symbols of the four Evangelists—the winged man, the winged lion, the winged ox and the eagle, in its upper part is the coronation of Our Lady in Heaven and, in the lower half, the Last Judgment. The rose is completed by the orders of the celestial Hierarchy, angels waving censers or playing on musical instruments and so forth. In the lancets are the thirteen Apostles, each holding his proper symbol and, except St Paul, with a scroll inscribed with a sentence of the Creed. Their canopies, some of which have small figures of saints round their tops, are three-sided with pendants. Below the Apostles are saints—SS. Louis IX, René and an unknown bishop—and the donors to whom we have referred.

This immense window, which contains 124 compartments, illustrates three principal characteristics of the Perpendicular style—reduction of intensity, as compared with Decorated work, in the coloured parts, increased use of white and yellow glass and elaboration of pattern work. Indeed, it may be said to be a white and yellow window heightened with colour; for colour is, in the main, confined to parts of the drapery, the curtain backgrounds of the figures, the nimbi and smaller fillings-in of the tracery.

A good idea of the preponderance of white and yellow glass in Perpendicular work may be got from the panel of Louis II of Anjou, which we illustrate. All is white and yellow except the curtain, which is green with violet medallions, its top border and side doublings being white and yellow, the sword-scabbard, which is red, and the field upon which the Angevin fleurs-de-lis are painted, which is, of course, blue.

These figures of donors are of great interest, for, apart from the fact that they are thought by some to be portraits—a doubtful supposition—they illustrate the history of France in the 15th century, contemporary costume and, by the heraldry—fine, bold designs—on shield and surcoat, they shew the alliances of the great French houses of those days. Observe that none of these figures are identified by their names: their coats-of-arms were sufficient for that purpose in the 15th century, for everybody understood heraldry.

We notice a novel use of the yellow stain in this

window—for touching up the high-lights of the face, such as the tip of the nose, the chin and the eye-brows. Finish is shewn principally in the comparatively minute diaper work in the head-dresses of the female figures, in the crowns, in the curtain patterns, and in the words of the prayers inscribed in the open books.

It is to the Perpendicular period that we must look for the earliest existing examples of painted glass in dwelling-houses and other secular buildings, for, although there can be no doubt but that painted windows were to be found in domestic buildings long before that time, and, probably, from the earliest period to which painting on glass can be referred, there are few or no remains older than the latter part of the 14th century to be seen to-day. Evidence of domestic use of painted windows in the reign of Edward III may be found in Chaucer's writings. In the "Book of the Duchesse," speaking of his own house, he says (line 321):

> "Sooth to seyn, my chambre was
> Ful wel depeynted and with glas
> Were al the windowes wel y-glased,
> Ful clere, and nat an hole y-crased,
> That to beholde hit was gret joye.
> For hooly al the storie of Troye
> Was in the glasing y-wroght thus."

We may, therefore, safely assume that picture

windows were to be found, in plenty, in the houses of well-to-do folk in mid-14th century days, and, if so, that they had long been common in the castles of the greater nobility and in the guild-halls of London and other towns. Figures representing ancestors or historical personages, such as the nine —two intended for Earls of Mercia and seven for Earls of Chester—in 14th century armour, originally at Brereton Hall, Cheshire, and afterwards removed to Aston Hall, Birmingham (although these particular figures were not painted until the 16th century), or those formerly at Warwick Castle and Arundel Castle, would be set up in the great hall of a castle or manor-house, while smaller figures of Our Lady and the Saints, under canopies or in panels, would be placed in the windows of chapels or oratories.

Later in the style we find that heraldry has largely taken the place of figures for the windows of secular buildings, although there are many recorded instances of figure subjects of late date, such as those of the Fettiplace family at Childrey, Berks., set up in 1526. The usual style of heraldic glazing for the great hall of a manor-house was an adaptation of the *belt* system of canopies. A large, boldly designed shield, with helmet, crest and mantling, and, if appropriate, supporters and crown or coronet, was set in the centre of each lancet, forming a belt across the window. All the heraldry was properly coloured and the white and yellow backgrounds usually consisted of alternate diagonal rows of rectangular quarries decorated with some small device—a family badge, monogram of husband and wife, or such-like—and white glass on which was painted the family motto. Our illustration—the arms of Henry VI and his wife Margaret of Anjou in the hall at Ockholt, Berks.—is a good example, painted about 1450, of this kind of domestic painted glass.

Towards the end of the reign of Henry VI shields became very varied in shape, and they usually shew the lance-rest, a piece cut out of the dexter side of the shield just below its top corner. The old plain shield, the widened heater shape, was, however, always in use, and often shields, when without helmet and crest, were encircled by wreaths, made of leaves, an entwined branch, with foliage or a scroll turned round a stick.

An illustration of the system upon which quarry-ornaments were designed is afforded by some quarries at Faulkbourne Hall, near Witham. They are decorated with a design made up of two family badges—the Stafford knot and the black-laced belt of Fortescue—and may be assumed to commemorate the marriage, probably about 1520, of Henry Fortescue, then lord of the manor of Faulkbourne, with

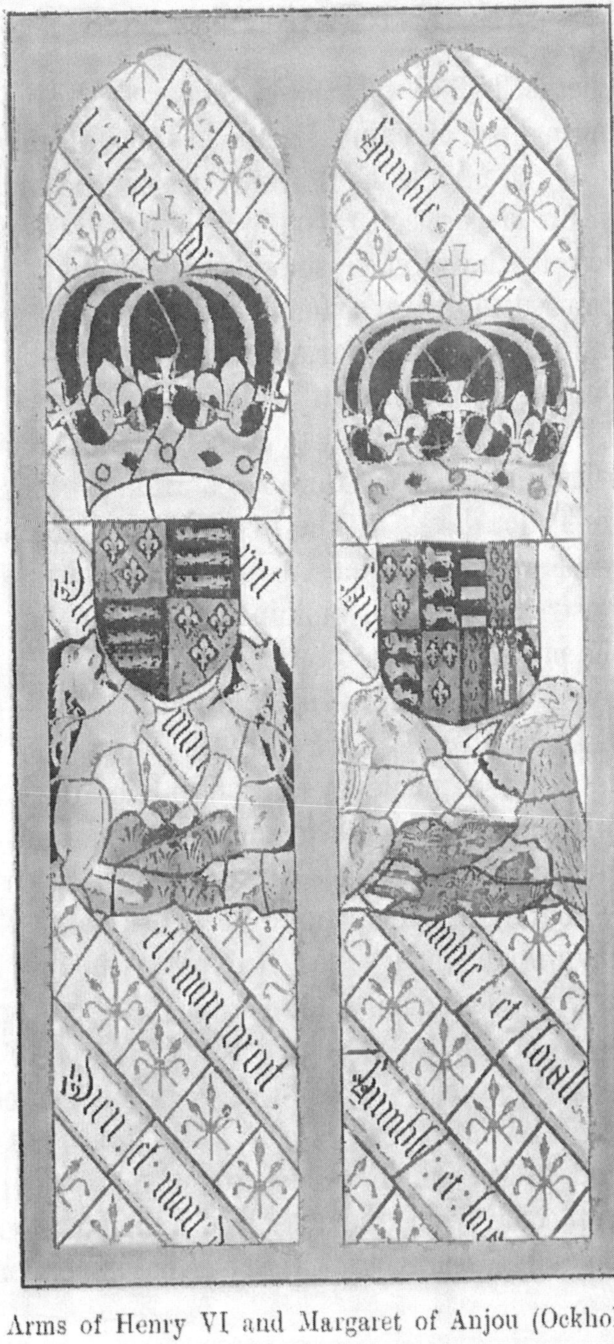

Arms of Henry VI and Margaret of Anjou (Ockholt)

Elisabeth Stafford. This old house, too, can shew an unusual use of painted glass, but one quite in the spirit of the Middle Ages, which deemed nothing too lowly for decoration. The upper part of a large window in the kitchen shews quarries upon which are painted, in brown enamel heightened with yellow, cooking utensils and various articles of food.

One may wonder what became of all the painted glass, of which there must have been an enormous quantity, in the monastic houses after the Dissolution in Tudor days. In the first place, no doubt, the old windows were, in most cases, taken down before the destruction of the buildings and sold; but how did the purchasers dispose of them? The price paid for the old stuff was usually absurdly low, as we know from several entries in the surveys of the religious houses made by the officials of the Court of Augmentations. One instance may suffice: two windows of the abbey of Kirkby Belers, Leicestershire, containing 160 square feet of glass, which would, probably, have cost to make, in the 15th century, not less than £160 (present-day currency), was sold for £1 6*s.* 8*d.* (equal to £13 6*s.* 8*d.* of our day), and 120 feet of painted glass in the choir fetched £1. As there is very little old glass in England to-day which can reasonably be supposed to have come from the dissolved religious houses, we can only assume that the purchasers exported it to the continent. If this assumption be correct, the interesting question arises as to how far the sudden throwing upon the continental market of so vast a quantity of painted glass may have been responsible for the state of things in France described by Bernard Palissy, himself a glass-painter. He tells us that, in the later years of the 16th century, painted glass was so little esteemed in France that it was hawked about the country by dealers in old clothes and such like refuse. In any event, it is difficult to account, otherwise, for the almost total disappearance of the painted windows removed from the churches, chapter-houses and other parts of old English monastic houses after their dissolution.

Although throughout the Middle Ages there were native glass-painters in England—probably as many as of any other craft, wood-carvers, wall-painters, or what not—yet it seems likely that most of the designs and patterns used by English artists came from the continent. We see in English village churches general designs similar to, and often even patterns in diapers, borders and quarry ornaments identical with those found in continental cathedrals. For example, the large floral pattern behind St Peter in the north transept window at Le Mans cathedral is the same as that used for the backgrounds of all the figures in the tracery at Sheering. It would be strange, indeed, when we consider the close relationship which existed between the British Isles and the mainland all through the Middle Ages—the constant passing to and fro of merchant, craftsman and ecclesiastic, bringing, not only the news of the day, but French and German songs and music, architectural ideas, fashions in clothes and illuminated books—strange it would be if notions, and even identical patterns, prevalent on the continent in the matter of painted glass had not come over with the rest.

Such a copying of continental methods and designs had always been, but, as the Perpendicular period neared its end, considerable numbers of foreign glass-painters, mainly Flemish, came over to, and settled in, England. They were encouraged by Henry VII and his son Henry VIII, and there can be little doubt but that the glass-painters called, in contemporary documents, "the king's painters," were, though not all of them Flemings, associated together under Flemish direction and that they used Flemish, German or Dutch designs in their work.

While upon the subject of foreign designs, we may say a word or two with regard to that much discussed piece of glass-painting—the east window at St Margaret's church, Westminster. It represents *the Crucifixion of Our Lord*, with the two thieves on either side. Above are angels holding the instruments of the Passion, and, in the side-lights, are kneeling figures the identity of which is, by no means, clear, although they are commonly said to be Henry VII and his Queen, Elizabeth of York. Above the male kneeling figure is St George and over the saint is a red rose with a white one in pretence upon it, while above the lady we see St Catherine and the arms of Aragon—a golden pomegranate in a green field.

The story usually told is that this window was intended as a present from the magistrates of Dort to Henry VII, and that pictures of that king and of his queen were sent to Dort for the purpose of securing accuracy in the kneeling figures; that, before the window was finished, Henry VII died, and, when it arrived in England, it was given, or sold, by Henry VIII to the canons of Waltham Holy Cross, who placed it in their church. After the Dissolution, the story goes on to say, the window was removed by the king to New Hall, near Boreham, and that, after divers vicissitudes, it was ultimately purchased by the parishioners of St Margaret's, Westminster.

Clearly, as the window stands, the kneeling figures cannot be meant for Henry VII and Elizabeth of York. The lady might be, and probably is, Catherine of Aragon with her patroness St Catherine and her paternal coat-of-arms. As to the male figure, the most likely supposition seems to be that it is intended for Henry VIII. Some have suggested Prince Arthur, his brother, Catherine's first husband, but it is hardly likely that Henry VIII would have set up the window in his chapel at New Hall—a favourite residence of his—had this been so. Perhaps the true tale may be that the window was, originally, intended to contain figures of Henry VII and Elizabeth, but that the plan was, after that king's death, altered by the substitution for them of Henry VIII and Catherine; or, again, even a more likely story seems to be that the window is not the one intended by the Dort folk for Henry VII, but another window altogether, simply a gift to the canons at Waltham Abbey by Henry VIII, who, in his early days, was a constant visitor there. The probability of this last suggestion is increased by the fact that the window is distinctly late in style, highly developed as to its light and shade, and may well have been painted about 1525.

A noteworthy feature of Perpendicular work is the growth of naturalism in landscape backgrounds of picture panels. In early examples such scenes are mostly painted on white glass heightened with yellow, the sky being pot-metal blue, or red and blue alternately and often diapered. Later on, distances are more naturally drawn on light blue glass and carefully shaded with yellow, while the sky, which is shaded to suggest clouds, is often dark blue above and light blue below. A similar tendency appears in the drawing of figures—they are rather short than tall, perhaps the result of putting them under canopies—which have lost the constrained attitudes of the Decorated period and assume an easy and natural pose.

Borders round white and yellow quarries are, in the earlier years of the style, much the same as those of the Decorated period, usually alternate pieces of white and yellow and coloured glass with designs on them in brown enamel, but as time went on, Perpendicular borders got narrower, and, in very late examples, there are none.

Lettering was very much in evidence in Perpendicular work, long explanatory extracts from the Vulgate, or, oftener, the Biblia Pauperum, being frequently written on panels above or below a picture. Examples are the two side west end windows at Fairford. Small letters are still black-letter, but capitals are Lombardic and are sometimes stained yellow and cross-hatched with small leaves in them—a tendency towards illumination.

CHAPTER V

RENAISSANCE (1547—1603)

ALTHOUGH we have taken the middle of the 16th century as the date for commencement of the Renaissance period, we must not forget that, even from the beginning of the second half of the 15th century on the continent, though not until later in England, the influence of classical models can be traced in architecture and its auxiliary crafts. In glass-painting we have prospective signs of change in that tendency to naturalism which we noticed in Perpendicular figure drawing, in the introduction of classical details in the canopies of the later part of the period—*e.g.* in the windows at King's College, Cambridge, in the more exact drawing and shading of landscapes and in the lights and shades of drapery. But, so long as glass-painters worked along the old Gothic lines—using pot-metal colours, yellow stain and brown enamel only—these tendencies were not overpoweringly apparent, and it is a fact that the closing years of the Perpendicular period, the first half of the 16th century, saw the perfection, so far as breadth, harmony and contrast of colour and the play of light and shade are concerned, of the art of glass-painting. The painter on glass had, as far as we can see to-day, attained to his highest plane by about the year 1535, after which his work began to lose effectiveness through his fruitless attempt to carry contrasts of light and shade beyond all reasonable limits by the use of deeper, and ever deeper, masses of brown enamel. The result was loss of transparency and an appearance of weight and opacity. It is, of course, impossible to say how the art would have developed had the old system of work been adhered to and had the glass-painter resisted the temptation to over-do contrasting effects. What actually happened was that, just when the art was losing its essential features—simplicity and transparency—a new force came into play, which, by encouraging facility of execution, helped the craft down the road to ruin.

This was the discovery, or, at least, the coming into general use—for it is very doubtful by whom or when the discovery was made—of enamel colours, whereby the painter was, at a stroke, freed from the limitations imposed upon him by the old pot-metal system. Instead of the laborious process of cutting his local colours, as it were, out of sheets of pot-metal, he applied them, like ordinary paint, in a fluid state, with a brush, on white glass. The number of pieces of glass to form the window being independent of the number and size of its coloured parts, the whole composition could be painted on a single sheet of glass and much lead-work thereby saved. All that can, with certainty, be said about the invention of enamel-painting on glass is that it came into general use about the middle of the 16th century and succeeded, during the ensuing hundred and fifty years, in largely superseding the pot-metal process.

A consequence of the use of enamel colours was disregard for lead-work as an adjunct to design. In pot-metal work the lead must follow the outline of every separate bit of colour, but not necessarily so in enamel work, for any number of different colours can be painted on the same piece of glass. As the enamel painter would naturally wish his picture to be as little broken up as possible, the tendency was to use large sheets of glass varying in shape with the painter's convenience, so that, in a Renaissance glass-painting, we usually find the lead lines running all over the composition with very little regard to the outlines of the subjects depicted, and, in some cases, the window is made up of large squares of glass of almost uniform size. In small pictures, the whole painting would be on a single sheet of glass.

Enamel glass-painting is seen at its best in small compositions, which, in effect, means that it is better adapted for dwelling houses than for large public buildings. The beautiful little circular medallions—scenes from Biblical history or classical tales, heraldry and such-like—which form a distinct type of Renaissance glass-painting, illustrate this. They are painted in various shades of brown running into red, flesh tints are properly indicated, the yellow stain is freely used and bits of bright colour are sometimes here and there introduced. The medallion is surrounded with a border in brown enamel—a running rose branch, perhaps, with heraldic roses, yellow centred, at intervals. Several such medallions, one over the other, would be leaded-up in each light, with a border—architectural or heraldic, and coloured—and floral fillings-in, in much the same style, except for the difference in amount of lead-work, as that in which the Norman and Early English medallion windows were arranged.

An interesting, though incomplete, series of such little pictures may be seen in the south window of the chapel of the Hospital of Our Lady and St Thomas of Kent at Great Ilford. As the stonework of the window is Decorated Gothic, of course these Renaissance panels are out-of-place where they are, but they have been there for many years, probably since the 17th century, and are conveniently placed for study. Three are figure subjects, *Our Lady visiting St Elizabeth*, *Joab slaying Amasa*, and what looks like *Lot warned by an angel to leave*

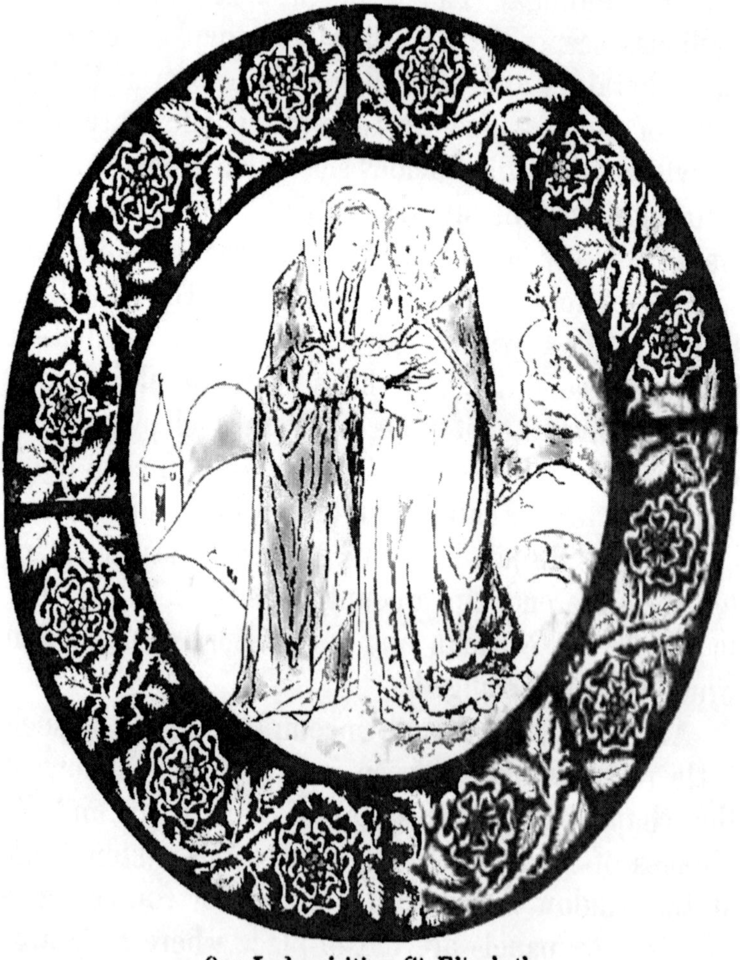

Our Lady visiting St Elizabeth

his house, and the remainder are coats-of-arms, including the shield of the Emperor Charles V.

These medallions, one of which is dated 1577, are unequal in design and finish and that of *Our Lady*

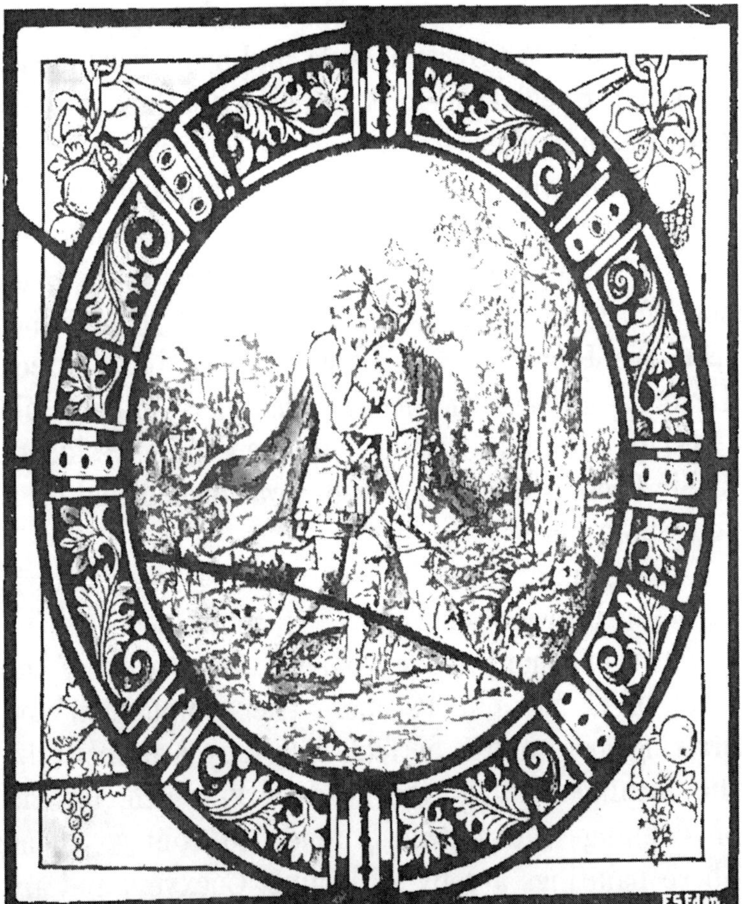

Joab slaying Amasa (Great Ilford)

and St Elizabeth is much faded. The *Joab and Amasa* is, however, a very beautiful piece of work, the flesh shading is highly finished and the landscape background—a mediaeval city with water and mountains—is delicately painted and reminiscent of the old Flemish painters. The heraldry, too, is good, bold work in the German style, and has a few touches of red. Special interest attaches to these panels, because they shew us the sort of picture glass with which the windows of domestic buildings of the Renaissance period were glazed, and for which that style is adapted. As far as it is possible to discover, the Ilford medallions seem likely to have come either from Sir John Gresham's house in Lombard Street, London—the sign of *The Grasshopper*—or from old Gresham House in Bishopsgate, the London residence of Sir Thomas Gresham, when it was dismantled prior to demolition.

Interesting examples of Renaissance domestic glass in brown and yellow are to be seen at the Château of Chantilly—44 panels with stories of the loves of Cupid and Psyche. The composition and drawing are almost perfect, but they are spoilt by the arrangement of the lead-work, which, instead of defining the outlines, tends to confuse them. These paintings are by a Fleming, Cocxyen, and are dated 1542.

Is it too much to hope that architects may, in time, come to adopt this brown and yellow medallion style for the windows of the many Renaissance buildings which are set up to-day in our cities instead of the meaningless patterns, usually *l'art nouveau*, in lead-work and white glass—the only recommendation of which is cheapness—which they commonly affect?

As confirmatory of our idea about the proper use of this style, we may refer to the churches of St Nicholas and St Pantaléon at Troyes in Champagne, which are entirely glazed with it. Seen upon a large scale, as in these churches, the style is distinctly disappointing and we realise that brown and yellow alone will not do for the windows of large buildings. Decided colour in masses is necessary to give strength to big transparent designs.

As it is obvious, having regard to the religious troubles of the 16th century, that we cannot expect to find native glass-painting in England for church purposes during the second half of that century, we must look abroad for examples. At Montmorency church, near Paris, is a fine series of Renaissance windows dated 1523—63. We notice the absence of borders, which, indeed, tended to disappear in late Perpendicular work, and, also, the importance of the figures of donors relative to the subject matters of the windows. Rather more than one-half of the lower lights are given up to kneeling figures of the donors, the Constable Anne de Montmorency, his wife and children. To take one as a sample of the rest: in the upper half of the central lower light is the Good Shepherd with the Holy Lamb and, on either hand, in the side-lights are Our Lady and St John. Below these are the Constable kneeling at a prayer desk, St Anne his Patroness, standing by. Behind him are his five sons—kneeling figures in armour with sur-coats of arms, one of them helmeted and the others having their helmets on the ground. In the tracery lights are, in the centre, the Montmorency arms—16 blue eaglets on a gold ground—supported by angels, above the shield a typical Renaissance feature, a cherub's head, and, on either side, a mailed hand grasping a sword entwined with a scroll bearing the words "nos apia" in Roman letters.

Interesting, as well for workmanship as for subject —the story of the world from its creation to the Sacrifice upon the Cross—is a window in the Lady chapel at the church of St Mary Magdalen, Troyes. In 25 pictures the painter sets forth the tale, which begins in the lowest tier of panels. First, in four panels, the world, as a rotating ball, is being fashioned by God the Father, who, in cope and triple tiara, stands by its side. In each panel the globe is represented in a more finished form, until, in the fourth, it appears complete. Then follow Adam and Eve in the garden, their fall and its consequences, the Old Testament stories, Abraham's sacrifice, the Israelites in the desert, the lifted-up serpent and the rest. The

Annunciation, Our Lady's visit to St Elizabeth, the Nativity and the visit of the three kings continue the story, which is finished, in the topmost tracery light, with Our Lord on the cross between the two thieves, St Mary Magdalen embracing the cross and our Lady and St John on either side. Below them, in the tracery, are pictures of the betrayal of Our Lord and His entombment, and, in the smaller lights, angels and bishops. From the small, crumpled drapery folds one gathers that this window is Flemish and its date is about the middle of the 16th century. A remarkable feature is the stonework of its tracery which runs into the form of a large fleur-de-lis, in the central leaf of which is the Crucifixion.

As to Renaissance *Jesse* windows, the general design of this type of window, necessarily remained the same as in previous styles, the principal variations being in the treatment of the vine, the branches and leaves of which became more natural, and in the figures of kings, which were often portraits, easily recognisable, of contemporary princes, in some cases, no doubt, donors. The *Jesse* in St Stephen's church, Beauvais, is, perhaps, the best known example of this practice: there we see portraits, among others, of the Emperor Charles V (1516—56), Francis I (died 1547), and his successor Henry II (died 1559). Although, on the whole, so natural in treatment—as witness, in particular, the great lily in the tracery from which Our Lady, holding the Divine Child, springs—the huge blossoms from which the half-length figures of kings issue are conventional in the extreme. Coloured backgrounds for *Jesses* being then in fashion, that at Beauvais is blue.

At Sens cathedral is a brilliant *Jesse* window, with red background, which contains a feature not always understood—a donkey on one of the branches. Grotesque as it may seem to the modern mind, the presence of this creature is quite in accord with Catholic tradition, which has always honoured the animal which carried the Founder of Christianity in triumph into Jerusalem. In the cathedral at Caudebec is a *Jesse* in which the figures are full-length, a return to the earlier type. At Rouen, in the churches of St Maclou and St Vincent are *Jesse* windows with white branches on blue grounds, and, in St Vincent's is, also, an interesting variant of the *Jesse* type; the vine springs from St Anne, mother of Our Lady, instead of from Jesse.

Another curious use of the genealogical tree is seen in the *wine-press* type of window. Instead of Jesse at the foot of the window is Our Lord's Body bruised in the wine-press, whence His Blood falls into a chalice. From His breast, or, sometimes, from the chalice, springs the vine, which bears, not Our Lord's ancestors, but those born of His teaching—His spiritual descendants, as it were—the Apostles and saints. The best known example is the window painted by Linard Gonthier in Troyes cathedral, in which the vine springs from Our Lord's breast and from its flowers issue the Apostles. This window is dated 1625, but, having regard to the excellence of its colour scheme and its workmanship—quite equal to the best 16th century work—we mention it here. There is also a fine *wine-press* window in the church of St Étienne du Mont at Paris, one of twelve enamel-painted panels by Robert Pinaigrier one of the best known 16th century glass-painters. Its vine bears figures, like so many of the *Jesse* windows of that day, intended to represent reigning sovereigns—the pope, the emperor, the kings of France and England and bishops and cardinals. At the church of St Faith, Conches, may be seen another style of *wine-press* window. Our Lord Himself is crushing grapes in the press, the flowing juice from which takes the place of His blood in the more usual composition.

We have, already, referred to the tendency, noticeable in the Perpendicular style, for figures of donors to usurp an unduly important position in picture-windows. One of the best illustrations of this bad custom is the painting—the descent of the Holy Ghost at Pentecost—in one of the many 16th century windows in the church at Montfort L'Amaury, near Versailles. The window has two long lights and the lower part of each light—fully a quarter of the whole—is occupied by a kneeling figure of a donor. The subject represented is quite subordinated to the donors. Our Lady and the Apostles, though well drawn and grouped, take quite a second place, and, owing largely to the sharpness of the perspective, they seem to be disappearing into the background. This window is a good example of Renaissance work and it makes us realise how far we have travelled from the Decorated period. Leaving out of consideration the moral aspect of the donor's question, we find no borders, no foliated tracery, no bold single figures under canopies, no trellissed or quarried background and no repose. Instead we have classical architecture —the waggon head vault resting on pillars and entablature of Roman composite style,—the sharp perspective, the distance seen between the pillars, all typical of the Renaissance and all excellent in their proper setting—an easel picture or tapestry, or, perhaps, a wall of a classical building. As glass-paintings, the Montfort L'Amaury windows are failures.

As we have already noticed, the 16th century saw a great increase in the use of painted glass for secular purposes. In England, the splendid palaces which were then set up by the Tudor kings and by the new nobility (who rivalled their sovereigns in extravagant magnificence)—Whitehall, Hampton Court, New Hall, Audley End, Wanstead and

Somerset House, and the lesser dwellings which were erected up and down the country by knight and squire—Shipton Hall and Benthall Hall, Shropshire, Lake House, Wilts., and Barlborough Hall, Derbyshire, among many others—the windows of all must, originally, have been glazed either with quarries and heraldry in the old manner or with brown and yellow picture panels like those at Ilford.

For window painting on a large scale in secular buildings during this period we must, however, again turn to the continent, especially France, where among many other examples, we find at Troyes, in the eight windows of the great hall of the Library, 32 panels, painted by Linard Gonthier, depicting all that happened at Troyes when Henry IV of France visited that city in 1595 and the coat-armour of most of those who there and then foregathered.

CHAPTER VI

THE SEVENTEENTH CENTURY AND AFTER

As we might suppose, from the terms of Queen Elizabeth's Ordinance requiring plain glass to be substituted for coloured glass in churches and for the destruction of all glass-paintings of a superstitious character, little or no picture glass for religious purposes was painted in England during her reign or for some years after. The craft of the glass-painter did not, however, wholly languish during that period, for it is certain that the demand for heraldic glass progressively increased from mid-16th century days to the end of the 17th century. And not only for secular buildings, for it became the fashion to substitute for the devotional subjects combined with heraldry, which had filled the windows of chantry chapels, the coats-of-arms, usually elaborately quartered, of the new families which had obtained possession of the lands of the dissolved religious houses, chantries and guilds.

Many illustrations of this custom might be given. At Great Parndon, in the chancel, is a mutilated shield, very well painted on white glass in enamel colours, shewing the arms of William Cecil, first Lord Burghley, and his second wife Margaret, daughter of Sir Anthony Cooke, of Gidea Hall, Romford, to whom he was married in 1546. The shield has been releaded in modern times, with the result that the quarterings, of which there are twelve, are in hopelessly wrong order, and fragments from other windows have been mixed up with the heraldry. Lord Burghley did not die until 1598, and we may safely assign the date of this glass to the closing years of the 16th century.

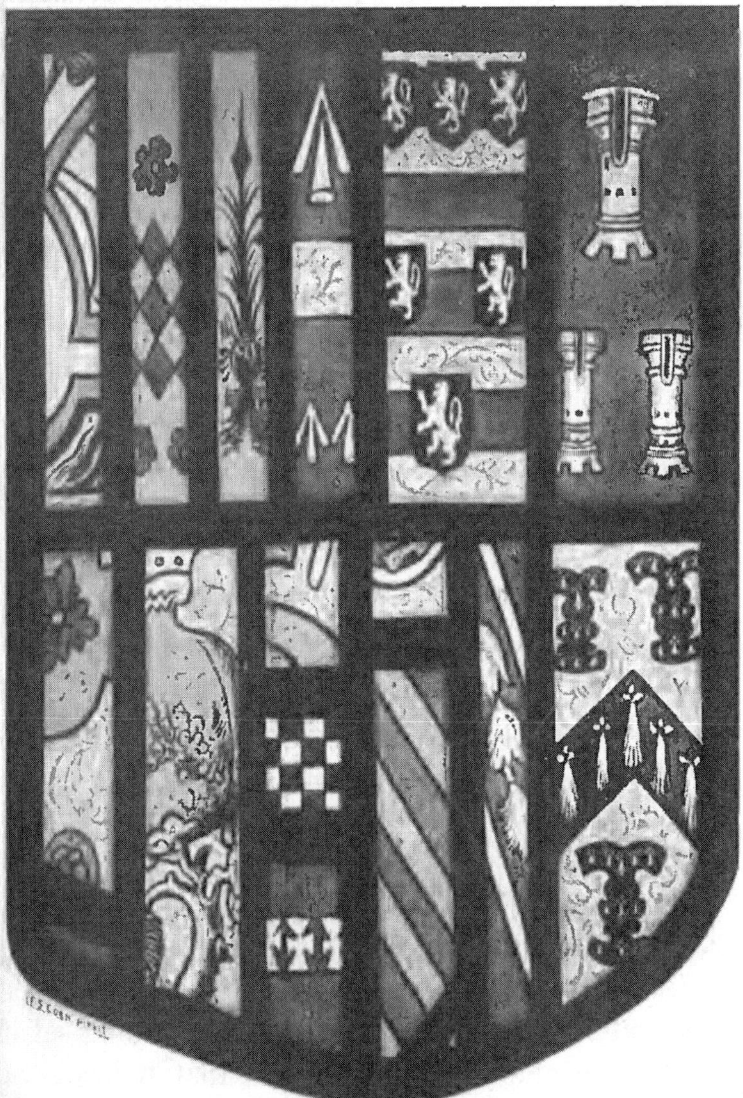

Arms of William Cecil, Lord Burghley (Great Parndon)

A very pretty bit of heraldry in enamel colours, also illustrative of the practice with regard to chantry chapels to which we have alluded, is the shield (there are three others relating to him) of Emanuel Wollaye at Latton church, near Harlow. The arrangement of the design is simple, the charges are well spaced and the diapering of the white glass —the *flanches* and the woolsacks—is refined and delicate. The woolsacks—of course, a pun on the name—are on a green field and the wolves—another pun, perhaps—are blue on white. This Wollaye shield and its fellows are now leaded into plain white glass quarries in the east window of what was, formerly, the chapel of the Holy Trinity and Our Lady on the north side of the chancel, but is now used as the vestry, and there can be little doubt but that they occupy the place formerly held by a religious picture and the coat-of-arms of the founder of a chantry in Latton church.

Uffington church, Lincolnshire, can shew another case of this sort in the arms of Trollope impaling Sheffield in the north window of the north chancel chapel.

Towards the end of the reign of James I, however, a revival of glass-painting for church windows set in in England and it cannot be said that it has ever, since that time, except in Commonwealth days, entirely ceased in the land, although 18th, and the

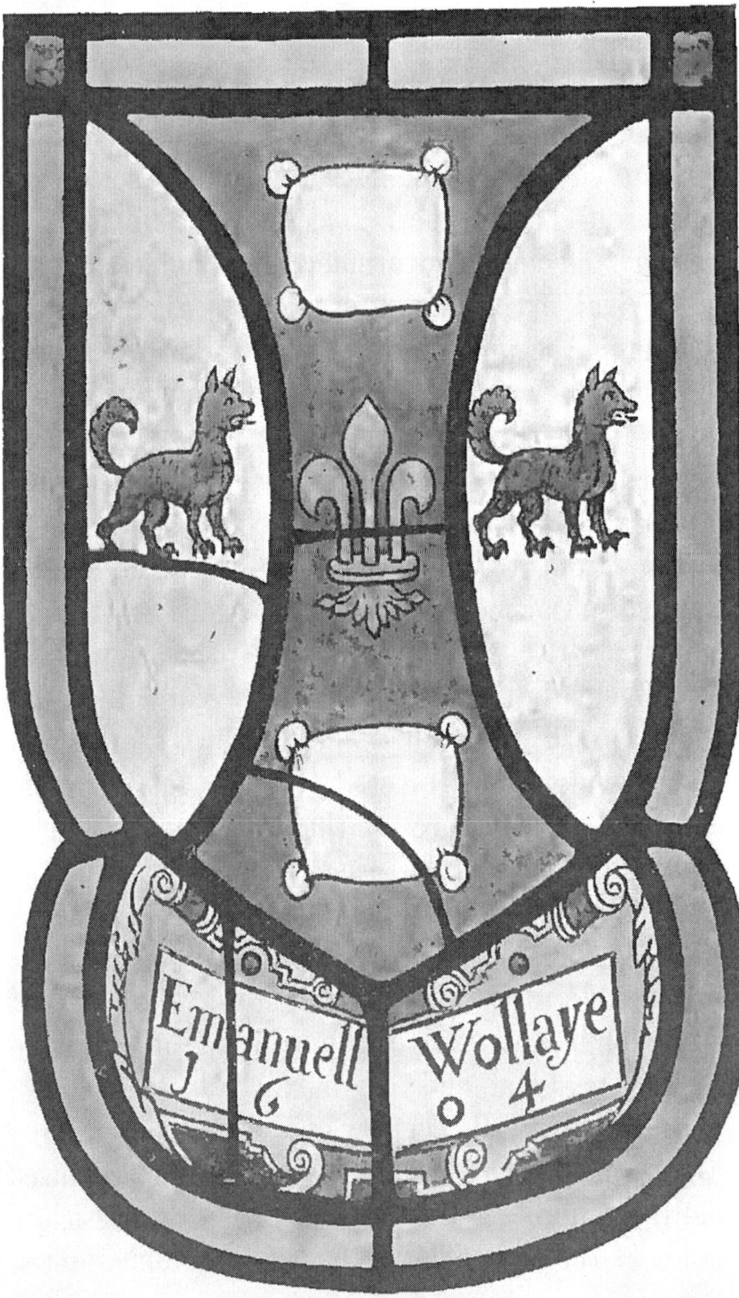

Arms of Wollaye (Latton)

greater part of 19th, century picture-windows are very poor things judged from the standpoint of the use painted glass is intended to serve. Archbishops Abbot and Laud, differing as they did in ideas of theology and church government, both helped forward this revival by patronage of Flemish glass-painters, who again began to settle and work in England. The best known of them were Baptista Sutton and the two Van Linges, Bernard and Abraham, many specimens of whose work, signed and dated, may be seen to-day—especially in Oxford Colleges. At Wadham College chapel, built in 1613—an interesting example of Jacobean Gothic—the windows are contemporary with the building, and the east window, soft and rich in tone, is by the elder Van Linge, and is, often, said to be his finest known work. The chapel windows at University College, set up in the reign of Charles I, are by the younger Van Linge, who also painted the windows (except the two westernmost on either side) of the chapel at Queen's College. One specimen of his work, too, has been left by modern restorers in a window at the west end of the north nave-aisle of the cathedral at Oxford—a picture of Jonah and the gourd.

During the 17th century the *figure and canopy* design continued in use, the details—often coloured—of the canopies being either classical or classicised Gothic of the style affected by Sir Christopher Wren in his restorations of Gothic buildings. But the most usual type for large windows was a picture extending over all the lower lights and, often, into the tracery, set in an architectural framework of the style which we noticed at Montfort L'Amaury. Sometimes, figures of donors were beneath the picture. Most of the work of the Van Linges at Oxford is of this character, with landscape backgrounds and much blue and rich olive green in the colour scheme. The windows at Lincoln's Inn chapel, London, saved by Archbishop Laud from destruction as superstitious and idolatrous, are either by one of the Van Linges or by a painter of their school. They are, for the most part, figures under canopies with donors' arms at foot, and are extremely rich in colour. In the west window are considerable remains of its original glass, among them the arms of Sir William Noy, the unpopular attorney-general of Charles I.

The tendency in the painting of flesh was to colour it naturally; lips and cheeks were tinted red, the iris of the eye blue and the eye-ball was shaded. Inscriptions were in Roman characters, and initial letters were often ornamental and stained yellow.

When the war between Charles I and the Parliament broke out, the Van Linges left England, but English painters, trained in their studios, seem to have carried on their methods of work. Henry

Giles, of York, who, in 1687, finished some of the uncompleted work of the younger Van Linge at University College chapel, is believed to have been one of their pupils. The east window of this chapel —the Nativity—is entirely Giles' work, and may be taken as an illustration of the extent to which the technical part of glass-painting had, in his time, deteriorated. For, so badly must the enamels have been prepared, that they have almost completely perished, leaving the pot-metal colours and yellow stain intact.

A great defect—want of clearness in the lights—is noticeable in enamel glass-painting all through this period and, indeed, down to modern times. The main cause—one easily got rid of—seems to be the custom of laying a thin coat of white enamel paint over the back of the window. It is this practice, based apparently on the utterly erroneous idea that the proper office of window glass is, not to admit light, but to form a screen on which to paint a picture, which produces that peculiar effect, observable in all enamel-painted glass, suggestive of the idea that the window is made of porcelain.

To Flemish influence may, perhaps, be due the existence of other English glass-painters of this century, although it may well be that there had been no break in the succession of the English schools of glass-painting, so far as heraldry and similar decorative work were concerned, even during the Commonwealth.

Besides heraldry, there was a fashion in the 17th century for portraits of eminent persons—kings, pious founders and so forth—to be painted on glass within small circles or wreaths. At Magdalen and Wadham Colleges, Oxford, are such little pictures of Charles I and his queen, and at Brasenose and St John's are similar paintings of their founders. At Harlow church, also, in the north transept window, in which is much good heraldic glass, principally of Tudor date, are portraits of Charles I and his grand-daughter, Queen Anne, the king's picture being curious in that it shews a celestial crown by the side of his head. Such portraits as these are to be found, also, in private dwellings, a good example being a head with heraldry at Northill, Bedfordshire, which is signed by the painter, "J. Oliver f. 1664."

On the continent the old devotional subjects continued to furnish material for the glass-painter. A very favourite style was an extension of the use of bright colour to the small medallions to which we referred in the last chapter, combined with greater variety in their shapes and surroundings. Often they were oblong, set in a frame of classical architecture with figures of saints at the sides and small sacred pictures and arms of donors at the top and bottom. Several of these would be set, one over the other, in a single light, with Renaissance borders and fillings-in of white and yellow glass. The borders were usually grotesque Renaissance in design—a mixture of vases, scrolls, wreaths, fauns, satyrs and so forth. The little pictures themselves were painted in enamel colours on a single piece of glass, but the architectural coloured setting was usually pot-metal shaded with brown. At Lambourne church, in the chancel, are five such little pictures, brought in the 18th century from Baden, which convey an excellent idea of this style, though they are without their white and yellow borders and settings. Each picture was the gift of a separate donor, whose name, office and arms are set forth at the foot of the panel. One of them we illustrate—*The adoration of the Shepherds.* The whole is painted in enamel except the entablature and the bases of the pillars, which are ruby. Notice the candle held by St Joseph, its halo like a palm-leaf fan, the sheep on the floor by the cradle and the quaint child-figure of Our Lady standing by St Anne, for, by a curious combination of two stages of the history, which is common in German art, the Virgin is represented as still a little maid, while St Anne holds in her arms the Divine Child already born of her. Observe, too, above St Anne the seated figure of the donor—as one supposes it to be—Herr Melchior Abeltin, in his robes of office. Though delicate in workmanship and rich in colour, these panels offend against all

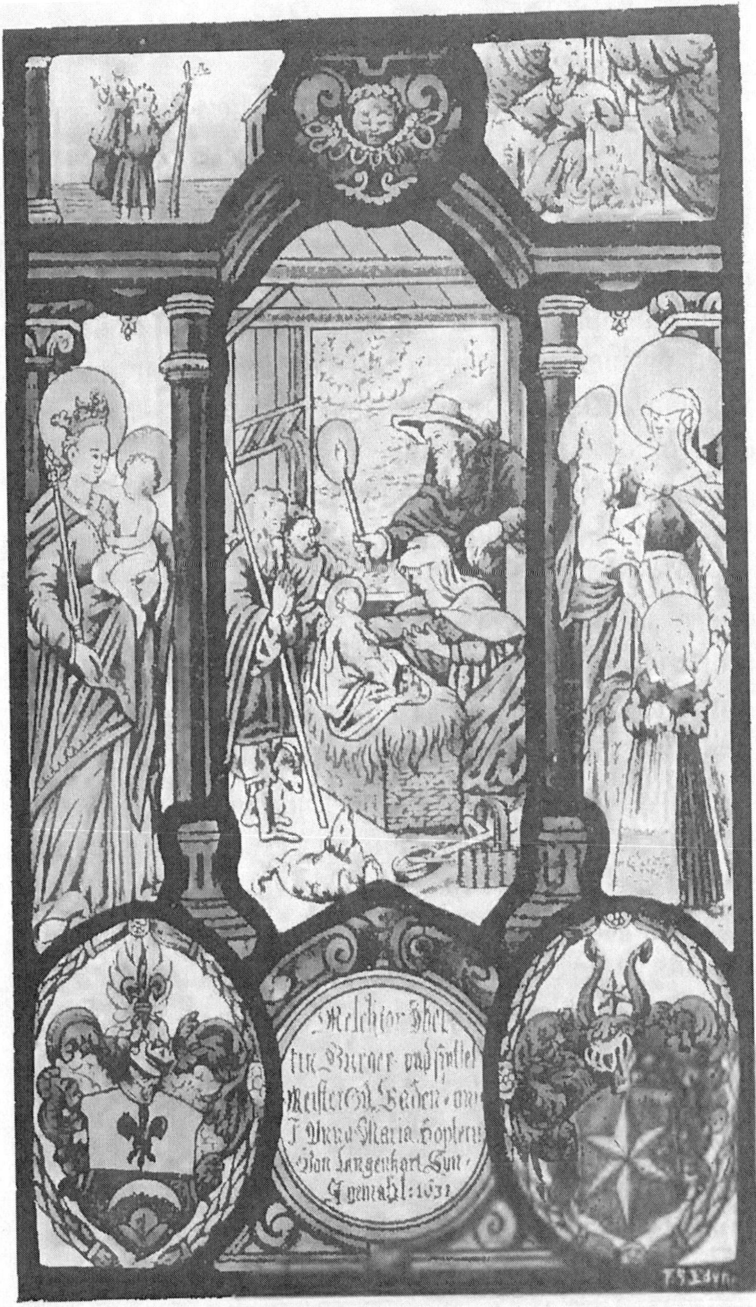

The Adoration of the Shepherds (Lambourne)

rules of the art of glass-painting. They are too small, when viewed from below, to be effective as helps to devotion and the colours of the pictures, owing to the absence of dividing lead-lines, run too much together to give the effect of the old mosaic windows. The glass-painters of the Renaissance, by their neglect, or ineffective use, of lead-binding for outlines demonstrate its value for that purpose.

For domestic buildings in Renaissance style—for hall and staircase windows, top-lights in dwelling rooms and such-like—enamel-painted shields, set in scroll-work, are very effective and appropriate, and there are plenty of good specimens of 17th century work left to serve as models. At the old Pyed Bull Inn at Islington, long ago destroyed, where, says tradition, Sir Walter Raleigh at one time lived, were several 16th and 17th century heraldic glass panels, among them the arms of Sir Francis Drake and those of Raleigh himself. Above Raleigh's shield was a tobacco-plant with sea-lions, while below were parrots, a grey one and a green, all emblematical, perhaps, of Raleigh's world-wanderings and of his fondness for tobacco.

There is a very elaborate piece of heraldry of the early part of the 17th century at Noke Hill church, near Romford—it was brought from elsewhere—shewing the quartered shield, with helmet, crest and mantling and the Garter, of Francis Manners, sixth Earl of Rutland.

An interesting, though not uncommon, instance of the survival of a feature of one style in work of a subsequent, and essentially different style, is to be found, in the north chancel window at Ilford Hospital chapel, in a small quartered shield of Dennis set within a boldly drawn wreath—a contrast to the rest of the design—suggestive of the Perpendicular style. In the wreath, however, is an incongruity, for, whereas its main feature is a purple chaplet, the clasps, white and yellow glass, are decorated with grotesque Renaissance patterns instead of the simple floral design—such as a rose or marguerite—of Perpendicular days. In the tracery of this window is a typical example, dated 1631, of 17th century heraldic painting, clearly English work—the arms of Ward, with three quarterings and two small side shields, and helmet, crest and mantling,—all set amidst fruit and flowers in a light blue ground. Among the panels, already described, in the south chancel window of this chapel is a pretty piece of heraldic painting, probably French, of the 17th century. The field of the shield is cobalt blue and the leaves and fruit around it are naturally coloured—green, purple and yellow: a pastoral staff, without a mitre, behind the shield indicates that the arms are those of an abbot.

By the end of the 17th century, glass-painting

had nearly reached its lowest point, and, after the traditions of the Van Linge school had died out, there is very little in its records worthy of notice until the revival of the art about the middle of the 19th century. Of that revival and of the progressively excellent work which has followed it, we do not propose, now, to speak, beyond observing that the success of modern glass-painters in their craft seems to be in proportion to the study which they have given to pre-16th century glass, to the fidelity with which they have adhered to ancient methods and models and to the extent to which they have imbibed the spirit which animated the workers of Gothic times.

Nevertheless, a few words upon 18th century glass-painting may not be out of place. At the beginning of the century the Price family were known as glass-painters. There were two brothers, William and Joshua, and Joshua's son William. Joshua produced good work in the Van Linge style, the best known of his paintings being the east window at St Andrew's, Holborn, which represents *the Last Supper* and *the Resurrection.* With the excellencies—the richness of colour, the careful drawing and composition—of the Van Linge school, this picture has the defects of the same school, especially the heavy and overworked shading. It is, however, by a long way, the best piece of work done prior to the modern revival. The other Prices did nothing that will bear comparison with Joshua's work. In 1702 the elder William painted, almost entirely in enamel, the east window at Merton College chapel, and his nephew and namesake, in 1740, restored the 17th century windows on the north side of New College chapel. The Van Linge windows in Queen's College chapel were, also, restored by the Prices in 1717.

William Peckitt of York succeeded to the connection of the younger William Price, and he did a great deal of work in his day. There is a large window by him, designed by Cipriani—the British Minerva presenting Newton oddly enough to George III—in the library at Trinity College, Cambridge. There is very little pot-metal glass in this painting and the enamel colours are hatched in the style of the oil-painter.

A piece of glass-painting—much discussed by the savants of the day, Horace Walpole among them—is the west window at New College chapel, Oxford. It was painted (as already mentioned) by Thomas Jervais (died 1801) from designs by Sir Joshua Reynolds, and represents, in the upper part, the Nativity and, below, the theological virtues, Faith, Hope and Charity, and the four cardinal virtues, Prudence, Justice, Fortitude and Temperance. It is executed entirely in enamel colours.

CHAPTER VII

HERALDRY IN GLASS

THAT branch of glass-painting which longest resisted deterioration was heraldic work. One reason for this was the reserve imposed upon the painter by the rules of heraldry: he could not go beyond the four colours commonly used in the science—*gules* (red), *azure* (blue), *vert* (green) and *purpure* (purple), and the metals *or* (gold or yellow) and *argent* (silver or white). Black, of course, he had, but as for the little-used colours, *tenné* (orange) and *sanguine* (blood red), I count them as varieties of yellow and red respectively. In the use of the allowed colours he was bound, too, by rule: colour must not be placed on colour or metal on metal, but colour on metal and *vice versâ*. It is true that this rule was not always observed in continental heraldry, some authorities going so far as to deny its existence, and we have, in the arms of the Kings of Jerusalem (gold crosses in a silver field), a notable instance of such non-observance, but, on the whole, the rule has always held in practice.

Then, again, by the very nature of heraldic art—the shewing of objects, mostly very simple in design, on a flat ground—shading was barred, and we know that one of the most potent causes of the ultimate ruin of heraldic painting in general was the attempt to represent, by elaborate shading, charges on a shield as they are in nature.

Whether the origin of heraldry was the need for a means of recognition of a fighting man when his face was concealed by a closed head-piece, or whether it was derived from ancient Aryan customs or has some connection with fetish worship, it is certain that it began to take form, as an ordered system, about the time when closed helmets came into use. Thus the head-man, the lord around whose person the folk of a manor or district would rally in fight, would be recognised by the charges on his shield and banner, and his sons, and often his brothers and other relations, would adopt a similar design with differences. So, by long familiar use, a general recognition of the whole family by a certain heraldic device would spring up.

By some such process the means of recognition in war came to serve the same end in general social life, and what more reasonable than the idea that, when a man died, a sight of his shield in window or on monument would remind men of good will to say a prayer for his soul?

Besides this memorial aspect of the science it ultimately came about, as the result of disuse of defensive armour, that the value of heraldry, as a means of distinguishing one family from another, became its only *raison d'être*, and it developed into a complicated science the main object of which was the registration of family alliances. Thus arose the practice of quartering, which, beginning with the inclusion of the arms of husband and wife, side by side, in the same shield, grew at last to the much-divided shield, with, perhaps, as many as 50 or more quarterings, of Elizabethan times.

There is but little heraldry in glass to be found in the Early English style. Some pattern windows have shields, but they are more like ornamented divisions of the window than separate designs, as witness the shields of Clare, England and France (ancient, *semée of lilies*) in the east window at Selling church, Kent. The heraldry of the day was simple—a shield, seldom containing more than two colours in the field, with a single charge, such as a cross or a lion—and its simplicity was reflected in such coat-armour as we find in Early English glass. The shields are large, of the earlier heater shape—*i.e.* the sides curve inwards continuously from their tops—and one coat only is in each shield, for quartering had not been invented.

As the Decorated period developed, shields got

Arms of France (ancient), Selling

smaller and narrower and changed slightly in shape: the upper parts of their sides became parallel, at right angles to the top lines. Such shields, still without helmet or other accessories, we find in the upper parts of lower lights, set in white ornamented quarries. Often they are surrounded by narrow circular borders, made up of small roses or rings and dots, with coloured fillings-in between the shields and borders. The charges are always few and simple and boldly drawn, and sometimes, as in the Hornchurch chantry window, they are painted in brown and yellow only, without reference to their proper heraldic colours. Quartered shields, though never with more than four quarters, appear in this period, but they are not so common as impaled shields, *i.e.* shields divided vertically into two equal parts for husband and wife.

The usual arrangement is, say, a three-lighted window, with a picture-panel, or figure and canopy, in the central light, the husband's arms alone in the dexter light and those of the husband and wife impaled in the sinister. Shields were, in early Decorated work, seldom diapered, but after a time diapering was sparingly applied to the ordinaries—bends, chevrons, chiefs and so forth—and, in the later years of the style, we find the whole richly diapered.

When shields occur in tracery they are often

hung by the guige, or shield belt, from a branch or a rosette, and, in large tracery lights, they are set between leaves, within narrow borders, running into the foils, like the Berkeley shield at Westonbirt church. Impaled shields were, and are, used for ecclesiastical and other official arms—the official arms in the dexter half of the shield and the family coat in the sinister. Sometimes, however, connection with an office is indicated by a charge from the official arms being placed outside the shield containing the family arms, but within the composition, say, between the shield and a circular border running round it. An interesting example of this practice is the quartered shield in a window at Arkesden church, near Saffron Walden, of Thomas of Arundel or Fitzalan, successively Bishop of Ely, Archbishop of York and Archbishop of Canterbury. The arms of Fitzalan, *a lion rampant gold in a red field*, are in the first and fourth quarters, and *checky* (like a chess-board) *gold and blue*, for Warrenne, are in the second and third quarters—a true quartered coat. The shield is set between three crowns to indicate the bishop's occupancy of the See of Ely—the arms of which are *three crowns in a red field*—a circumstance which enables us to fix the date of this piece of glass between 1374, when Thomas became Bishop of Ely, and 1388, when he was translated to York. Another quartered coat of this period is at Little

Chesterford—the first and fourth quarters simply a blue and gold pattern representing a fur called by heralds *vair*, and in the second and third quarters *a fess between six crosses patonce—all gold in a red field*, for Beauchamp of Hache.

In the Decorated period, family badges—such as the bear and ragged staff of Warwick, the Percy crescent, the Hungerford sickle, the Dacre knot and so forth—begin to appear in painted glass, often on lozenge-shaped quarries. Also, we find rebuses, punning allusions to surnames, like Abbot Ramryge's device at St Albans, a *ram* with a collar inscribed *ryge*, or Abbot Kirton's at Peterborough, a *kirk* on a *tun* or barrel, or Archbishop Islip's name in a quarry ornament, which we illustrate.

Speaking generally, and without reference to a few particular cases, arms were borne, prior to the middle of the 15th century, only by the land-holding classes—the origin, in this instance, being military—and by great ecclesiastics. Rich merchants, however, needed something analogous to coat-armour, and so it became a custom for them to make distinctive devices for themselves by combining their initials with a cross and a triangle, and, often, with other objects, after the style of Sir John Gresham's mark, to which we refer later. These devices were called merchants' marks, and they are found, in plenty, used for all decorative purposes, carved in

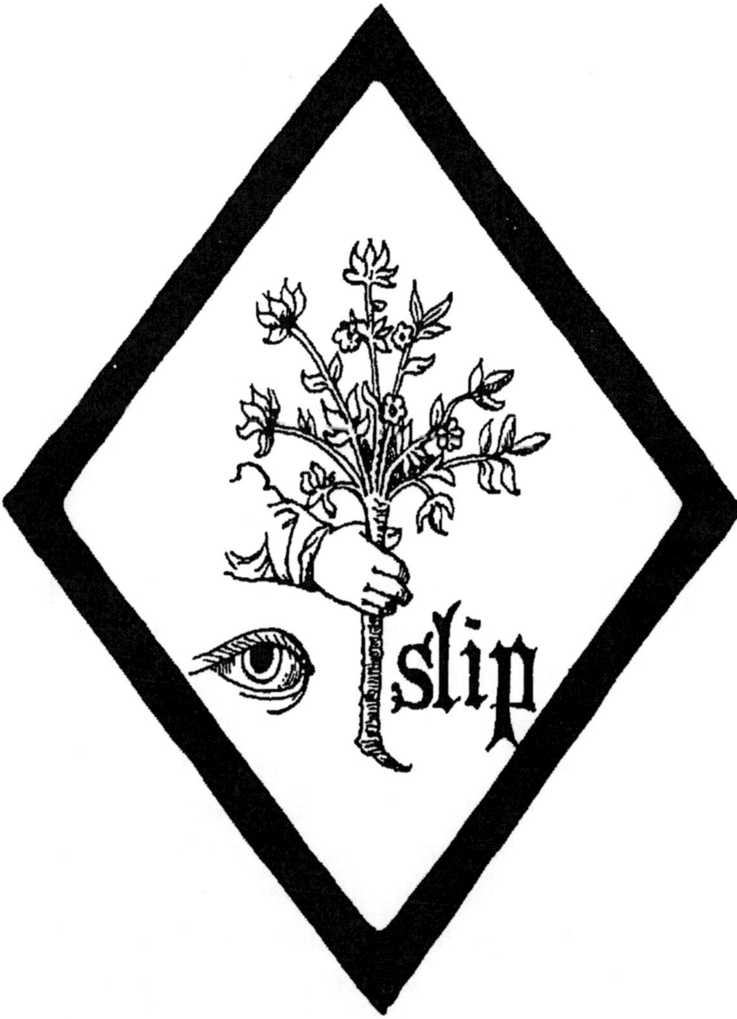

Punning device on quarry

wood or stone or painted on glass, from the 14th century onwards. In the poem *Pierce the Ploughman's Creed* (1394)—not by William Langland, though often attributed to him—mention is made of these marks in the description of a Dominican church:

> "Wide wyndowes y-wrought
> Y-wryten ful thikke,
> Shynen with shapen sheldes,
> To shewen aboute,
> With merkes of merchauntes
> Ymedeled betwene
> Mo than twentie and two
> Twyse ynoumbbred."

Perpendicular heraldry was a gradual development, mainly in increased richness of detail, from that of the Decorated period. At first, there was but little difference between the styles, but gradually diapering assumed more complicated patterns, and charges were drawn in bolder outline, with more attention to detail and, often, in grotesque shapes. Quarterings increased in number and full achievements became the fashion—helmets with mantling and crests, coronets, supporters and mottoes were added to the shield. The shield itself, too, tended to variety in shape, until, towards the end of the style, it is found in almost every conceivable form, a circumstance which paved the way for the floriated,

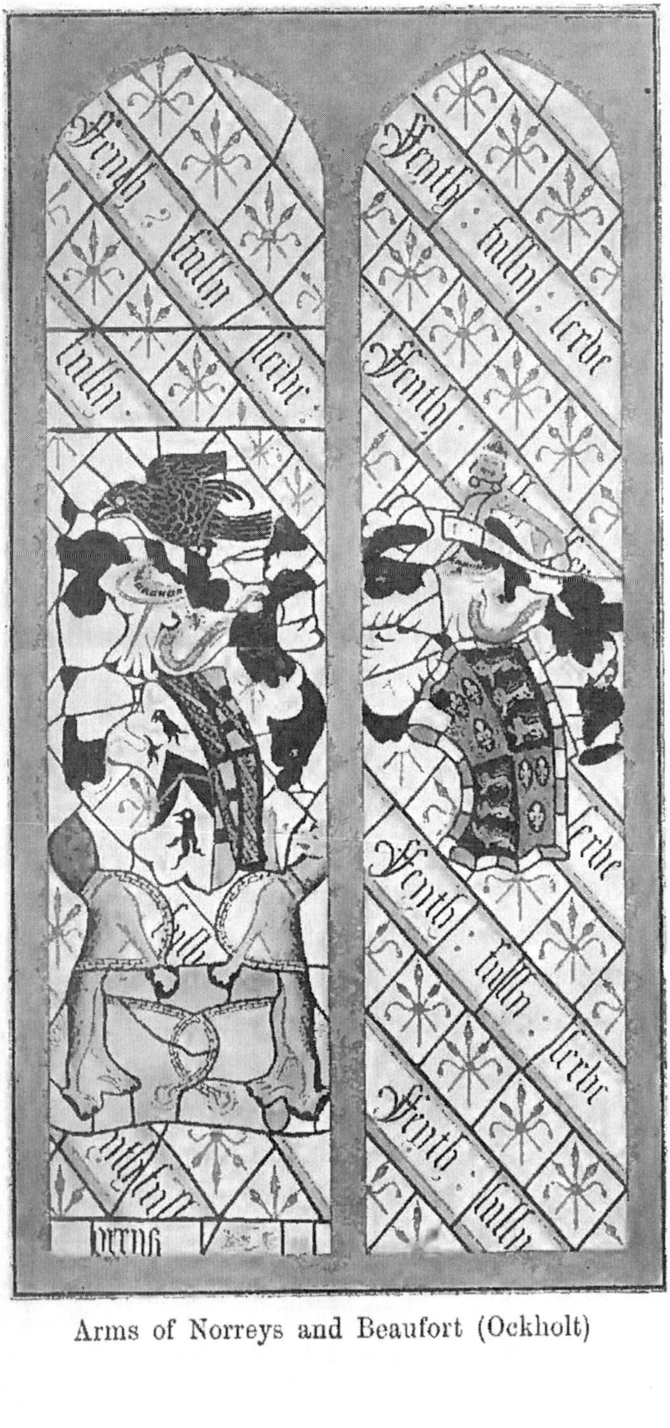

Arms of Norreys and Beaufort (Ockholt)

and quite non-heraldic, shields of the Renaissance and subsequent periods.

The complete achievement first appears in glass in England about 1450, but earlier abroad. Fine examples of this type are the arms in the Hall windows at Ockholt, already referred to. We illustrate two of these lights, shewing the arms of Norreys, probably of Sir Edward Norreys—and those of Beaufort—most likely that Edmund Beaufort, Duke of Somerset, who was beheaded at Tewkesbury in 1471. The plain shield, squarer in shape than the Decorated type, was still, however, used, in lower lights surrounded by border and coloured fillings-in and, later, by flowered wreaths, in panels below figure and canopy subjects, and in tracery lights supported by angels or hung by the guige. Punning allusions, too, were common, as in the wreath of peach leaves and fruit (each peach charged with the letter *é*) round the shield of Sir John Peché (1522) in Lullingstone church, Kent.

Large tracery lights often had shields in their centres, with scrolls inscribed with mottoes on the quarries. An instance is the shield of Cardinal Beaufort (died 1447) in a quatre-foiled tracery compartment of one of the refectory windows at the Hospital of St Cross, near Winchester. The shield is ensigned with a cardinal's hat, the cords and tassels of which mingle with the quarries, mottoed "A honeur et lyesse," in the two side and bottom foils.

Perhaps the most prominent of the uses to which

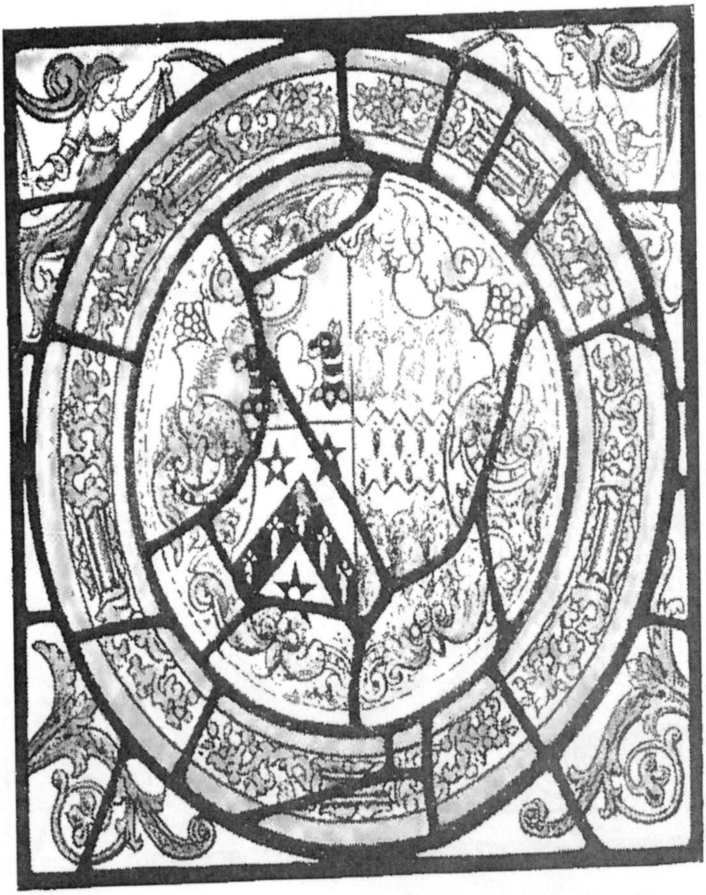

Arms of Sir John Gresham (Great Ilford)

heraldry was put in the glass of this period was decoration of the surcoats of armoured figures, as the donors at Le Mans, and, less commonly, of women's dresses and ecclesiastical vestments. Borders, too, were, as in the Decorated period, often

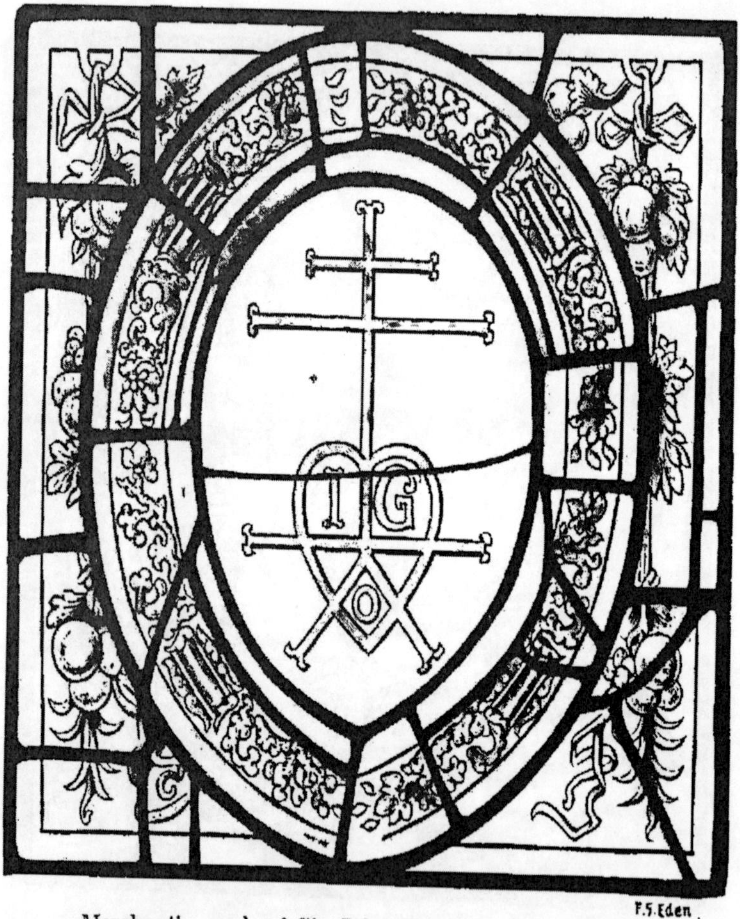

Merchant's mark of Sir John Gresham (Great Ilford)

heraldic, made up of badges, charges from a shield, ostrich feathers, monograms and so forth, alternating with coloured glass, and the custom of using brown enamel heightened with yellow stain alone, without other colour, was increasingly prevalent.

With the 16th century came signs of the Renaissance, and, by 1540 or thereabouts, Gothic had largely given place to classical forms for shields and accessories, and we get such monstrosities—from the heraldic point of view—as the panel at Ilford hospital shewing the arms of Sir John Gresham, Kt. (died 1555), and the oval-shaped shield, or cartouche, on which his merchant's mark is painted. The quarries decorated with the Gresham badge—a grasshopper—are fair specimens of the poor kind of thing which the ornamented quarry had become. The letters I and M in the mouths of the grasshoppers stand for John and Mary—Sir John Gresham and Mary his wife.

After 1700 heraldic glass-painting rapidly deteriorated and soon became the wretched travesty of heraldic decoration—enamel painted on thin, clear glass—which we often meet with in 18th century churches, and we can hardly say that the revival of glass-painting in modern times has, as yet, restored heraldry in glass to anything approaching its ancient standard.

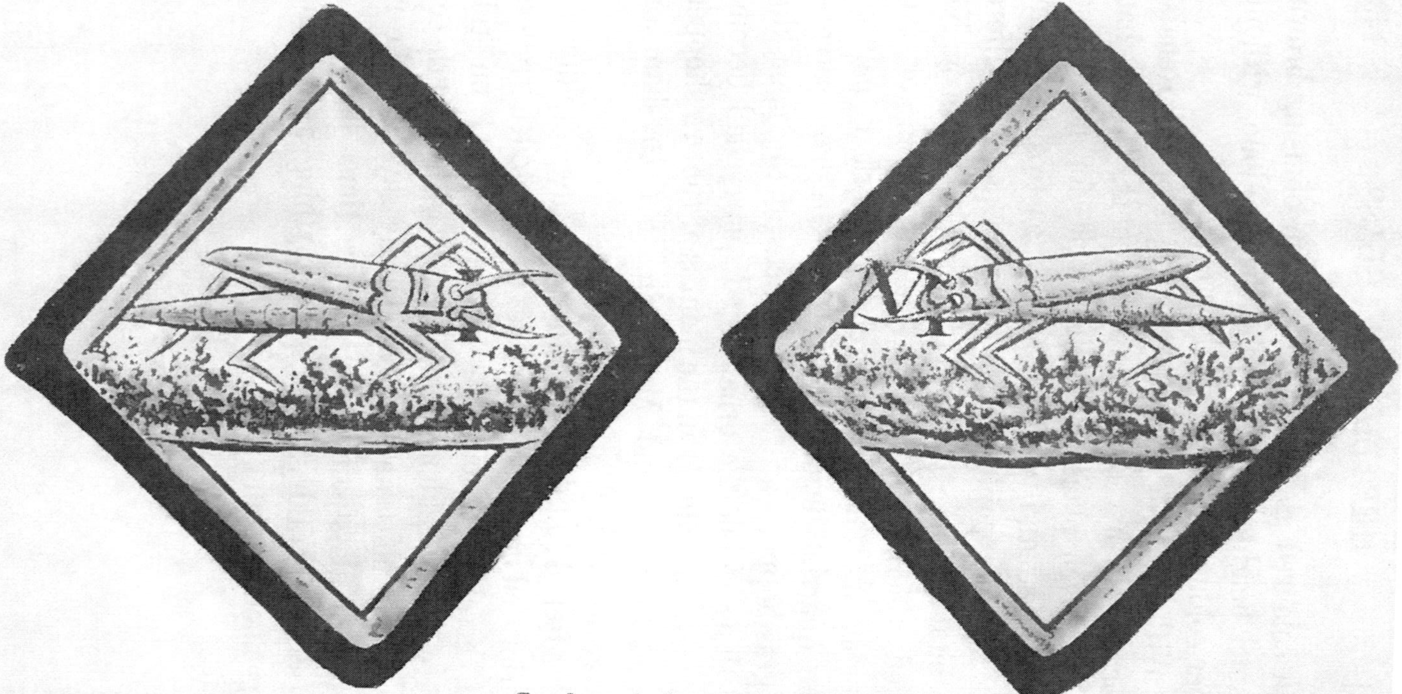

Gresham badge (Great Ilford)

CHAPTER VIII

LAST WORDS

We have already referred to the fragmentary state of the greater part of the old painted glass which has survived to our times. There is abundant evidence—a large volume could be filled with it—that, since the 16th century, destruction here and abstraction there of the ancient painted windows have been continuous. Take one or two cases.

St Martin's church, Stamford, is a very museum of old heraldic glass, and we might, at first sight, conclude that here, at least, the windows have been carefully preserved. In the east window are more than forty shields of arms—episcopal sees, York and Lincoln, the abbey of Peterborough, the Prior of Durham, old baronial families, Marmion, Grey, Comyn and others. But enquiry would bring out the fact that the greater part of this brave show was brought to St Martin's from other churches—among others, Snape, Yorkshire, and Tattershall, Lincolnshire—in 1754 by Brownlow Cecil, Earl of Exeter, whose object seems to have been to give an air of baronial splendour to the church in which his ancestors lay buried. The spirit in which these removals were carried out may be judged of, if a writer in the *Gentleman's Magazine* (1821, Part II, p. 307) is to be trusted, from the fact that, after the painted glass had been removed from the choir of Tattershall church, the window openings there were left unglazed for fifty years, although the earl had promised to replace the old stuff with plain glass. The 18th century Earl of Exeter did no worse than many have done before and since his time, and it was certainly a fortunate accident that he set up his spoils in a parish church instead of in a private chapel.

To come nearer to our own times. When William Flower, Norroy king-at-arms, visited Rochford church, Essex, in the days of Edward VI or Elizabeth, he noted, in some of the church windows, among other ancient heraldry, the arms of Bohun. This Bohun coat was of peculiar interest as being the only memorial left at Rochford of the builder of the 14th century church which preceded the present Perpendicular structure. The Bohun who built the old church was either William de Bohun, Earl of Northampton (died 1360), third son of Humphrey, Earl of Hereford and Essex, or his son Humphrey, Lord Constable of England (died 1372). It is certain that the Bohun coat—the mere monetary value of which was very considerable—together with fragments of figures and canopies, scroll work and inscriptions, were in the east window of Rochford church when its restoration was taken in hand in 1862, and that, during that restoration, it was removed and has never been replaced. This is only one of many similar cases known to the writer, and, although it may be freely admitted that better ideas about, and a juster appreciation of, ancient painted glass are gaining ground over the country, yet there are, unhappily, still many—often people of influence and authority—who have not attained to correct views on the subject, and it cannot be said that the old painted glass in our churches is, speaking generally, so safe and secure from destruction or removal as one would like it to be.

The truth is that there is no effective authority to protect it. Legally speaking, the property in painted windows is in the churchwardens as representatives of the parishioners; but, if they are neither so well instructed as to be interested in them nor so scrupulous in duty as to preserve them, no one else can interfere—or, at least, is at all likely to do so—if the windows are destroyed or taken away. Then it often happens that the only old painted glass left in the church is in an aisle or side chapel belonging to a private person, usually as appurtenant to his house, and the churchwardens cannot legally interfere with it, even by way of needful repair. The powers of the churchwardens, also, so far as they do extend, are subject to control by the bishop, whose faculty is necessary to the removal of painted glass from the church windows, and it is to be feared that a faculty, in some cases, rather facilitates the destruction or loss of old glass than its preservation. For, when the mass of broken lead and small, dirty, lichen-covered pieces of glass, which together make up an old painted window—perhaps an Early English medallion of priceless value—has been taken, quite legally, under a faculty, from its setting and thrown on the ground amidst a heap of broken stonework and brick rubbish, of what use does it seem to be? And is the ordinary man very blameworthy if he takes small pains to preserve it or if he jumps at an offer, often made in such circumstances, to exchange it for modern glass?

What is the remedy for this unsatisfactory state of things? Clearly the appointment of local authorities—not the District Councils or any existing body—whose sole duty should be the care and preservation of all historical monuments older than 1700, including painted glass, within their districts. The area of jurisdiction of such authorities might very well be the Hundreds—ancient county divisions, the convenience of which for administrative purposes is not always recognised as it deserves to be—and they might, perhaps, be constituted somewhat like this. A council of twelve for each Hundred, six members of which should be elected by the District Councils within the Hundred, three elected by the clergy of the deanery or deaneries within it, two nominated by the council of the principal archaeological society of the county, and one by His Majesty's Office of Works.

For such a scheme to be workable, it would be necessary that the control of these local councils—call them Ancient Monuments Councils—over their subject-matter should be absolute, so that nothing, not even repair (except, of course, such as might be urgently required to save a monument of antiquity from immediate injury), could be done to an ancient monument without the consent of the council, signified in writing under its seal. Statutory provision for the safe-guarding of all public and private rights would, it is assumed, be made.

To facilitate the work of the councils, especially to enable them to maintain such actions and prosecutions as might at times be necessary, each Hundred Council should, by statute, be created a corporation, with perpetual existence and a common seal and with capacity to sue and be sued. The members of the councils should be unpaid, though it would, probably, be necessary to provide them with paid secretaries, for the work in each Hundred, if properly done, would take up the whole time of one man. The necessary funds for the work of the Hundred Councils might be provided partly by the County and District Councils and partly by Exchequer grant and voluntary contribution. Whether there should be an appeal from the decisions of the Hundred Councils to, say, the Office of Works, may be a matter for consideration.

A very necessary work, without which the councils would be of little use, needs immediate attention —the scheduling of the monuments to be placed under their care. In the case of painted glass, the schedules ought, if they are to be effective for purposes of reference and identification, to be supplemented by tracings of every piece of old glass, however fragmentary, included in the schedule. From the tracings, carefully finished and coloured traced copies should be made, the copies should be mounted and kept in portfolios at the office of each Hundred Council and the original tracings should be deposited in the Record Office. So far as other monuments (except brasses, of which rubbings would be taken) are concerned, they should be photographed, but photography is of little use for copying glass in detail.

The powers of the councils should be wide, and they should have unlimited discretion to deal with schemes for bringing into usefulness broken or fragmentary glass. Too often such glass, from which it is usually possible, if it be still *in situ*, for an expert to build up something very like the window of which it originally formed a part, is taken from its setting, leaded up with other fragments into a confused mass—a jumble window—and inserted in some out-of-the-way place, perhaps, in a tower window or a side window of the chancel. How much better would it be to make a new window around the old pieces—taking care to distinguish them, say, by gilding or painting their leads—than, by the jumble-system, to destroy their usefulness for ever? The Hundred Councils would go into all such questions and evolve plans for dealing with them.

Some progress, fortunately, is being made towards these good ends by the Historical Monuments Commission, whose work comprises the scheduling of all monuments of antiquity older than 1700. Hertfordshire and Bucks the Commission has already dealt with and the schedules of their antiquities, including painted glass, have been published. These county schedules, as they appear, when supplemented by such tracings and copies as we have suggested, would form the basis for the work of the Hundred Councils.

AIDS TO FURTHER STUDY

SOME who have looked through this little book may like to go further in the study of old painted glass. To them I would say, the best books on the subject are the nearest ancient cathedral and the old parish churches round about your own neighbourhood, wherever it may be. For it is a thing to be remembered, and one not always recognized, that, despite neglect and destruction, ample materials for first-hand study of old glass are still to be found through the length and breadth of England. You may see, in the average country church, glass of the same quality, design, and workmanship as in the cathedral; the same craftsman did both. The difference is in quantity and size of window: for, while the destroyer may have been at work in both cathedral and parish church since the 16th century, it is likely that a larger quantity of old glass will be found to have survived in the cathedral than in the parish church, though the latter may still shew enough painted glass of pre-18th century date to satisfy the reasonable needs of the student.

As, however, books have their uses as guides to practical work, we may mention a few which cannot be consulted without profit and to which the writer gladly acknowledges his own indebtedness. First, the four folio volumes of Mr N. H. J. Westlake's *History of Design in Painted Glass* (1881–94); next, Winston's *Styles in Ancient Glass-painting*, two volumes (Parker, Oxford, 1847), the standard books on our subject for English readers; then *Windows, a Book about Stained and Painted Glass*, by L. F. Day (Batsford, 1909), the late Rev. J. J. Joyce's *Monograph on the Fairford Windows* (Arundel Society, 1872), and, for the chapel windows of King's College, Cambridge, the short *Guide* by Dr M. R. James, now Provost of the College (Cambridge University Press, 1899). On continental glass we have, for Le Mans cathedral, *Vitraux peints de la Cathédral du Mans*, by M. E. Hucher (Paris and Le Mans, 1865); for Bourges cathedral, *Monographie de la Cathédral de Bourges*, by Fathers Martin and Cahier (1841); and for general books on glass-painting, from the French point of view, Le Vieil's *L'Art de la Peinture sur Verre et de la Vitrerie* (Paris, 1774), *Essai historique et descriptif sur la Peinture sur Verre*, by E. H. Langlois (Rouen, 1832), and Lasteyrie's *Histoire de la Peinture sur Verre* (2 vols., Paris, 1857).

An excellent sketch of old painted glass in the

cathedrals and great churches of northern and central France is *Stained Glass Tours in France*, by C. H. Sherrill (John Lane, 1908)—a book which indicates in its author a fine enthusiasm for ancient glass; and a standard German book is Dr Gessert's *Geschichte der Glasmalerei* (Stuttgart, 1839; English translation, 1851).

INDEX